I'm so thankful for the path that Lisa Leonard has walked, from perfection and performance toward connection and grace, and I'm thankful as well for her vulnerability and creative storytelling. Her journey is one that will resound with so many women.

SHAUNA NIEQUIST, *New York Times* bestselling author of *Present Over Perfect*

I've been inspired by Lisa Leonard both online and off for years, and reading her story only deepened my respect for the way she does marriage, parenthood, and business. I cried three times while reading *Brave Love.*

LAURA TREMAINE, blogger and podcaster

The powerfully vulnerable voice in which Lisa Leonard pours her story onto each page is disarming and poetic. This book will dig out all your insecurities and doubts, and through each poem and life lesson, it will remind you of your wholeness, your value, your beauty. An inspiration to any mom, business owner, partner, sister, or friend, *Brave Love* will take you on a beautifully introspective journey and leave a mark of gratitude and abundance in your heart.

JESSICA HONEGGER, founder and co-CEO of Noonday Collection and author of *Imperfect Courage*

With soulful vulnerability, Lisa Leonard shares her story in *Brave Love.* Through Lisa's prose and storytelling, I was immediately captivated by her journey and saw pieces of my own story. You will find yourself coming face-to-face with the doubts and questions you hold, as well as with the bright freedom we all seek. Lisa's words will make you feel understood and will bring hope that you will come to know more deeply the freedom and love that God has for each of us.

BRI MCKOY, author of *Come and Eat*

Brave Love is inspiring and vulnerable, and it will resonate with every mom, in whatever season of life. I devoured it. Lisa Leonard pulls back the curtain on her life, writing about the hard work of growing a multimillion-dollar business, the not-so-pretty parts of her marriage, and the challenges of raising a child with special needs. In addition to sharing the hardships she's walked through, her story offers readers the wisdom, grace, and joy she's found on the journey.

JESSICA TURNER, bestselling author of
Stretched Too Thin and *The Fringe Hours*

A must-read! *Brave Love* is gripping, honest, and uplifting. Lisa Leonard's journey is unlike most, yet incredibly relatable as she weaves a story that may initially appear to be a tragedy into an undeniable triumph that will touch and inspire the hearts of many.

MEG APPERSON, blogger at Four Fine Lives

I've long been a fan of Lisa Leonard Designs and her gorgeous jewelry. Along comes this shimmering jewel to add to her collection: *Brave Love*. Lisa does with words what she does with her jewelry. She makes you feel beautiful when all you had felt before was "not enough." Each page stirred something deep in me—a woman who suffers from the chronic condition of "not-enoughness." *Brave Love* is at once gentle and powerful, and I know it will awaken something within you too.

JENNIFER DUKES LEE, author of *It's All Under Control* and *The Happiness Dare*

You were written with love, composing body and soul. Each verse fits together. You are complete; you are whole. *Brave Love* is the perfect read to spur you on toward being your bravest, truest self. Lisa Leonard's story about embracing her inmost desires and dreams and letting go of the idea of "perfection" will encourage you that being fully you not only matters but will lead you toward something more whole and beautiful than you could ever imagine for yourself.

STACIE BLOOMFIELD, founder of Gingiber

The lessons Lisa Leonard shares from her own life journey are important, meaningful, and inspiring—giving ourselves permission to be who we really are, embracing our individual needs in the midst of family and work demands and the mess of everyday life, and speaking our own truth even when it's hard. The ways she is owning her story resonated with me on so many levels as a business owner, parent, wife, and friend. Definitely recommended as inspiration to reconnect with ourselves.

ALI EDWARDS, storytelling advocate and
business owner at aliedwards.com

Lisa Leonard's honest words about loving her family and herself are inspiring. Her vulnerability is a breath of fresh air. She courageously shares her struggles in motherhood, marriage, and career in a way that will encourage others to be brave in their lives too. Her story is one of finding her voice to speak up for what she needed and to believe she is worthy of love.

MEG DUERKSEN, blogger at Whatever

Lisa Leonard teaches us that brave love shows up. And she certainly showed up for us in this page-turning memoir. Because of her vulnerability, her graceful truth-telling, and her imperfect courage, I was able to find my own story and truth in her words. Thank you for reminding me that I am not alone on this journey to become brave love.

ASHLEY STOCK, blogger at Little Miss Momma

This book will change the way you give yourself grace as *you*—and as a mother, a wife, a sister, and a friend. It will remind you that you can show up for you while bravely loving the people who mean the most to you.

DANIELLE SMITH, founder of PrettyExtraordinary.com

Love others, love yourself—through Lisa Leonard's brave truth-telling of her own imperfect journey, she will empower you to see that you too are loved, valued, and worthy.

KRISTI QUILL, owner/artist at Barn Owl Primitives

Lisa Leonard has a gift for walking people through both her darkest and most hopeful moments with true heart and vulnerability. Her story is one worth reading and sharing with everyone you know.

ALLISON CZARNECKI, founder and editor of Petit Elefant, a lifestyle blog

Lisa Leonard is a shining example of someone who bravely steps into the places God is leading her—and learning more about herself, humanity, and God by doing so. I'm so thankful she bravely took the steps needed to write this book so that all of us have an opportunity to get a glimpse into her life, and in so doing we can also choose to be brave.

HEATHER AVIS, author of *The Lucky Few*

MAKING SPACE *for* YOU *to* BE YOU

LISA LEONARD

ZONDERVAN

Brave Love
Copyright © 2018 by Lisa Leonard

Requests for information should be addressed to:
Zondervan, *3900 Sparks Dr. SE, Grand Rapids, Michigan 49546*

ISBN 978-0-310-35230-3 (hardcover)

ISBN 978-0-310-63175-0 (special edition)

ISBN 978-0-310-35239-6 (international trade paper edition)

ISBN 978-0-310-35241-9 (audio)

ISBN 978-0-310-35231-0 (ebook)

The author is represented by Alive Literary Agency, 7680 Goddard Street, Suite
200, Colorado Springs, Colorado 80920, www.aliveliterary.com.

Cover design: Connie Gabbert Design + Illustration
Cover photo: Heather Gray
Photo insert background: PhotoDisc
Interior design: Kait Lamphere

First printing October 2018 / Printed in the United States of America

To Stephen, David, and Matthias—
I am grateful for our little family.

CONTENTS

AN INVITATION TO BRAVE LOVE

I used to think love was easy.

Love was kind and gentle and polite.

Love was kisses and hugs and togetherness.

And love is all those things—but much more too.

Love is honest and raw and messy.

Love breaks down and takes time to rebuild.

Love dies.

Love begins anew.

Love changes and grows.

Sometimes love is easy, and sometimes love is soul-wrenching.

Just because it's hard doesn't mean it's not love.

Much of the time, life is normal and beautiful. We hum along in a rhythm, thriving. But sometimes life is messy and ugly and downright AWFUL. There are times when everything feels wrong. I feel overwhelmed. I feel like a failure. I feel too many feelings too strongly. In those broken-down moments, I let myself be weak. I admit to myself that this is really, really painful.

Then I whisper to myself, *This is brave. This is love. This is brave love.*

This is what it looks like to give wholeheartedly to my husband, to my children, to my loved ones, to myself. This is what it looks like to love with my heart and my hands and all that I am. Sometimes it's raw emotion. Sometimes it's crazy and ugly and too much.

Sometimes love means staying when I want to run away.

Sometimes love means making space to be alone and regroup.

Sometimes love means yelling and screaming and laying everything on the table.

Sometimes love means listening quietly without judgment.

Sometimes love means working on myself so I can be more whole.

Sometimes love means working together so we can have deeper connection.

We live life together. We laugh, we sing, we explore, we're silly. But we also cry and scream and fall apart. We show our souls to each other—in all our amazing imperfection. We apologize and give each other grace. Lots of grace. We say it's okay to be honest and imperfect.

This is brave. This is love. This is brave love.

I am imperfect, and that's okay. My husband and my kids are imperfect. Love doesn't require perfection. Love is bigger than the hardest, ugliest stuff we are facing today. Love is filled with grace and covers over our imperfections.

My journey to brave love has been up and down, forward and backward. I have had to unlearn wrong thinking, learn new ways of thinking, practice and then practice more. I have had to become comfortable with being uncomfortable. I have had to engage in conflict when I wanted to smile and nod. I have had to face my biggest fears—not knowing what the outcome would be. There have been desperate moments and amazing victories. And I still don't have it figured out. I have so much to learn, so much room to grow.

This book is the overflow of my heart—my thoughts and stories—some so vulnerable I typed them with tears streaming down my face. Some chapters took weeks to write, not because I wasn't sure what to say, but because I was terrified to put these stories on paper.

I hope you will open your heart as you open this book.

I hope you will be gentle with me, as well as with yourself.

I hope you will resonate with my stories and feel seen and understood.

I hope we can journey together into dark places, as well as into beautiful places.

I hope we can be honest with each other and in that honest place find we are capable of so much more than we thought.

It's risky but necessary. And I believe that if we walk together and support each other along the way, we will find incredible things ahead.

This is brave. This is love. This is brave love.

Will you join me?

chapter one

THE RED BOWL

I grew up in a family with seven children. Our kid tribe consisted of three sets of twins and one single brother. The birth order sequence begins with my oldest brother, Daniel, followed by me and my identical twin sister, Chrissie; my two younger sisters, Ellen and Susan, who are fraternal twins; and my youngest brother and sister, Jeff and Jodee, also fraternal twins. From oldest to youngest, we are just three and a half years apart.

Poor Dan. I'm sure it was hard on him growing up without a twin when everyone else in the family had their other half. But I don't feel too bad for him now because he and his wife eventually had twin daughters of their own! Additionally, my twin sister and her husband adopted twin daughters. It's a little crazy and maybe hard to make sense of, but twins are extremely common in my family.

Aside from the twin factor, ours was a family much like the other families in our Southern California community. My mom and dad were hardworking people and pillars of faith in our conservative Brethren church. We went to church every Sunday morning, Sunday evening, and Wednesday evening. We attended every potluck, baptism, vacation Bible school, church picnic, and Christmas pageant.

My dad worked as a medical technologist and was an elder at the church, and my mom stayed home with us full-time until I was in junior high school. She packed our lunches, attended our school assemblies, volunteered as a room mom, did laundry, and grocery-shopped for a family of nine.

In addition to all the routine parenting tasks, my mom also showed her love for us through creativity and generosity. She sewed our Halloween costumes, clothes for my dolls, and beautiful pillows edged with lace that she sold at a local boutique. She decorated our home with well-chosen antiques she found at garage sales or thrift stores. When I was about eight years old, she completely redecorated the bedroom Chrissie and I shared. By herself, she hung beautiful floral wallpaper, put soft, new comforters on our twin beds, and then added her colorful, handmade pillows. She set up a little table in the corner where we could draw and color and organized our clothes into new dressers. When she had every detail just right, she brought Chrissie and me upstairs to see our new bedroom. I could hardly believe I got to live in such a lovely space!

When I was ten, my mom told me I could pick one piece of antique furniture from around the house and she would give it to me when I got married. I walked from room to room looking at different pieces—an armoire with beautiful scrolling woodwork and a large mirror on the inside, a painted bed with flowers across the headboard, a coffee table with just the right amount of scuffs and scratches to give it texture and charm.

I finally chose an old pine sideboard. It was a beautiful piece designed to both store dishes and serve food buffet style. It had a shelf on top, a plate rack under that, and a cupboard at the bottom. It was a light wood, sanded to a soft, matte texture. While many antiques came and went over the years, my mom was true to her word and saved that piece for me. It lives in our home to this day, displaying our brightly colored Fiestaware dishes and storing odds and ends. At ten years old, I chose well—I still love that antique sideboard and the meaning it holds. Someday, I hope to pass it down to the next generation.

I have so many fond memories of growing up in a large family. I especially loved summers in our backyard. We had a large, round, aboveground pool. That's where my siblings and I spent hours creating what we called "whirlpools." We ran the inner perimeter of the pool in the same direction, over and over again, until it created a current. Then someone, usually my older brother, Dan, declared it "done." That was the cue to stop running and enjoy the force of the current. Sometimes we grabbed hold of the edge of the pool with our hands and let the current carry our feet away from us. Or we tried to walk against the current, fighting it like salmon swimming upstream. Or we simply floated, letting the current carry us along. When we were all tired out, we climbed out of the pool, picked fresh plums off one of the backyard fruit trees, and lay down with our towels on the hot concrete to dry off. These days were the stuff of beautiful childhood memories. I can still taste the sweet plums and smell the wet concrete.

We were a house full of big personalities—all leaders and no followers. Even as kids, all seven of us were driven and hardworking. We had strong opinions and loved to joke around. We were also natural-born storytellers, always ready to share the crazy events of the day with whomever would listen. In a family of this size, you had to speak up to be heard. You also had to be quick and feisty if you wanted to sit in the "good chair." And if you didn't hurry to the table when the pizza arrived, there might not be any left for you.

My dad was intentional about using every opportunity to instill life skills into us. When I got my driver's permit at age fifteen, my dad taught me to drive in a huge, fourteen-passenger van. When I complained about the size of the vehicle, he told me he wished he had a semi-truck available. He wanted me to learn to drive all types of cars and trucks. Just because it was hard didn't mean it was bad. His message was clear: *Challenge yourself, push yourself.* By age sixteen, I could drive a stick shift and knew how to check the oil and fluids in my car so it didn't overheat. Strangely enough, there was one thing my dad never got around to showing me about cars—how to pump gas. One day, right after Chrissie and I got our driver's licenses, we were out in the car when we noticed that the fuel gauge was on empty. We pulled into a nearby gas station and had to ask a woman at a nearby pump if she would show us how to put gas in the car. She laughed as she demonstrated how to remove the gas cap, insert the nozzle, and fill up the tank. Then we checked the oil and water levels without her help. Between us, we had enough scattered skills to get around town.

It was my dad who usually made breakfast on school days. Sometimes he made scrambled eggs and cinnamon rolls—one of my favorites of his homemade breakfasts. Simply yum! However, there were also days when he made boiled prunes and oatmeal. Yuck! He had a sense of humor about having us eat different foods. I did not share his sense of humor. But he often made up for it by bringing us donuts on Sunday mornings. He worked nights at the hospital and would pick up a box of glazed and sprinkled confections on his way home. On Saturdays, we usually fended for ourselves and had cold cereal. That may not sound exciting—especially compared to boiled prunes—but I *loved* cold cereal. To this day, it is my go-to comfort food, Lucky Charms being my absolute favorite.

Saturday mornings—cold cereal day—began with a race to get downstairs. If you are one of seven kids, you want to be the first to choose what cartoon to watch, the first to help yourself to a big bowl of sugary goodness, and, if you happen to be the earliest riser, the first to nab the greatest prize of all—the red bowl. Mind you, we were not a family short on bowls. Our cupboard included an assortment of perfectly good bowls. There were blue bowls, yellow bowls, orange bowls, and even an avocado green bowl, but it was the red bowl that was coveted by all. I don't know why. I suspect that, at some point, one of us simply declared it to be the best. There was only one red bowl and we all wanted it. These are the politics of being a kid in a big family. When there isn't enough of something, you have to fight for it.

On a typical Saturday morning, I opened my eyes and jumped out of bed, hoping to be the first to the kitchen so I could secure the coveted red bowl. Most Saturdays, I was too late. But on a rare Saturday, I might be the first to the kitchen to pour my Lucky Charms into that cherished red plastic bowl. I loved the rush that came with victory. *I won the competition! I came in first place! I have what my siblings want, and that means I matter!* Of course, the thrill of victory was fleeting, but for those few minutes, I was on top of the world.

I'm still not sure why, but something changed when I was around eight years old. I woke up early one Saturday, but I didn't hop out of bed. I didn't race downstairs. I didn't dash to the cupboard to get the red bowl. I was tired. Fighting for the red bowl felt like too much work.

I'll just let one of the other kids have the red bowl, I thought. I'll use an orange bowl. It doesn't really matter that much. Maybe it's easier not to need or want something I can't have. Maybe that's what it means to grow up.

At some level, I stopped caring about the things I wanted. I let others have the things they wanted. I would go without. Like all those summer days spent in the pool, I reasoned that maybe it was easier to go with the flow than it was to fight the current. Maybe I should just settle for whatever I got.

Looking back, I wonder if this was the beginning of a pattern that would follow me well into adulthood, a pattern of setting myself aside. I learned early on to put my needs and wants way up on a high shelf. I tucked them away and decided they weren't as important as other people's needs and wants. I tried to stop hoping and wanting. If I needed less and wanted less, I might be able to find peace in the moment. I could avoid disappointment. Besides, wasn't it better to please others, to put them first and be content with less? I had been taught in Sunday school that good girls were quiet and obedient. They listened more than they talked. They wanted to please and serve others. They didn't argue or talk back. Good girls didn't cause conflict or trouble. And so that was how my young mind tried to make sense of it all.

On that cold-cereal Saturday morning, I took a big step toward avoiding conflict—and a big step away from myself. In the ensuing months and years, I would travel long and far down this road, ultimately arriving in a place where I was unable to identify my needs and wants at all. I would come to believe my needs and wants did not matter, at least not as much as everyone else's needs and wants. With practice, I would excel at making myself less so others could be more. I would make sure they had what they wanted first. And I would slowly disappear.

The desire to love and serve others sounds kind and generous—and it is. But the way I practiced loving and serving was less about benevolence and more about control. I wanted to control my environment and other people in order to have peace.

I believed if I could make others happy, they would love me. It was my way to earn acceptance and approval. Yet it never worked, at least not in any sustainable way. The only thing that happened when I put my needs and wants up on a high shelf was that I began to lose myself—the person I truly was on the inside.

This pattern continued as I entered my teen and young adult years. I did not show up. I did not speak up. I did not say what I thought and felt. I ignored tugs of desire. When asked what I wanted for dinner, I responded, "Anything is fine." I pushed down my needs and wants. I ignored my heart. After a while, I realized I didn't even know what I wanted or needed. So I started to take my cues from friends or siblings—to want what they wanted, to need what they needed. I said what I believed others wanted to hear.

I stopped being me and started being someone who could go with the flow, someone who gave up hope of ever having the red bowls of life.

Chasing the Shadows

God is good.
God is love.
I learned these truths when I was little.

His light surrounds me.
He watches over me.
I felt his presence from a young age.

I wanted to be good.
I wanted to please God.
I wanted to deserve his love.

So I worked hard
And tried to be good.
I felt his light behind me, like sun on my shoulders.
But shadows stretched out before me—
Dark shadows as far as I could see.

So I worked harder,
And I tried to be better.
His light was always behind me.
His presence was always with me.
He was always beside me.
But the shadows were always before me—
Dark shadows as far as I could see.

I worked even harder;
I tried to be better, perfect even.
Day by day, the weight on my shoulders grew heavier.
My back and legs grew tired.
My heart was weary and sad.
No matter what I did, it was never enough.
I could never overcome the shadows—
Dark shadows as far as I could see.

In my desperation, I dropped to my knees,
Buried my face in my hands and wept.
As tears rolled down my face,
I felt the warmth of God's light behind me.
"I'm sorry, God,"
I said with desperation.
"I tried so hard.
I wanted to be good.

I wanted to deserve your love.

But I could never overcome the shadows."

I felt him gently tap on my shoulder.

With empty hands and a broken heart,

I turned around.

I turned away from the life I knew;

I turned toward God.

His warm light overwhelmed me.

The glow of his goodness filled me with peace.

His love consumed me.

As I turned toward God, there were no shadows, only light.

He whispered to me,

"You don't have to work harder.

You don't have to be good enough.

You don't have to do it on your own.

I love you.

I have always loved you.

I am enough for you.

I have always been enough for you

Turn toward me with empty hands and a broken heart.

You will find what you need right here.

I will surround you with my goodness and protection.

I will fill you with my love.

I will shine my light and chase the shadows away."

chapter two

BEING A TWIN

I loved growing up with a twin sister. It was never just me; it was us. I was part of a set, which meant I wasn't alone. I had a sister who had been by my side since before we were born. We were one—one egg that then became two. Chrissie and I knew each other inside and out. Our lives were full of shared experiences, not to mention shared DNA. I was incomplete without my twin sister. As an adult, the only way I can begin to describe the unique bond of being a twin is to compare it to mother love. When my friends became first-time moms, they described feeling a deep, passionate love for their child they had never felt before. A love that was fierce and intense, rare and beautiful. The kind of love that enables a mother to do whatever it takes to love, nurture, and protect her baby. When my baby was placed in my arms for the first time, I thought, *I know this love. This is the love I have for Chrissie.*

When Chrissie and I were little, we often fell asleep side by side in the same twin bed. We each had our own bed, but we preferred to share. We were two pieces that fit together perfectly— salt and pepper, night and day, peanut butter and jelly. We would lie in bed together and make up silly songs. We sang them and laughed. We laughed because the songs were awful. We laughed because we loved being silly together. Everywhere we went, we were together—and for most of my childhood, I had Chrissie by my side.

As children, we were often asked two questions: (1) Have you ever switched places? and (2) If one of you is in pain, can the other one feel it? The answer to the first question is, yes, we switched places one time. In fifth grade, Chrissie and I joined Pioneer Girls at a church near our house. It was kind of like Girl Scouts—we sang, did crafts, and completed tasks to earn merit badges.

One week when our leader left the room briefly to get materials for a craft project, Chrissie and I switched seats. When our leader returned, all the girls around the table stifled giggles and tried to pretend everything was normal. Our leader looked a bit concerned and a little confused but proceeded with giving us instructions for the craft project. When she addressed Chrissie as "Lisa," we all giggled. When she called me "Chrissie," we all giggled again.

"What's going on?" she asked.

We quickly confessed that we had switched seats, expecting her to get a kick out of our little prank. Instead, she stood up from the table and looked back and forth between Chrissie and me as if she had been betrayed.

"That is *deceitful!*" she said with a raised voice. "You lied to me. You switched places at the table, and you lied about who you were."

Even as a kid I remember thinking she was overreacting. Part of me wanted to burst out laughing. Part of me felt ashamed. We were in trouble. We had done a bad thing. Our teacher wasn't in on the joke, and she probably felt foolish. That was the last time Chrissie and I switched places. The experience didn't turn out to be as fun as I had hoped.

It was one of those times I learned a lesson and mentally filed it away for future reference. *Ah, yes,* I thought, *good girls don't play tricks on other people. Good girls sit quietly and never give anyone a reason to be angry.*

The answer to the second question is also yes—when Chrissie is in pain, I can feel it, but not always in the way you might think. I remember one time at recess, a friend came running over to tell me Chrissie was in the nurse's office. She had stepped on a nail that pierced her foot.

How did I not realize this was happening? I should have known! How could I be playing at recess while my twin sister was hurting?

I ran to the nurse's office and sat beside Chrissie as the nurse cleaned her punctured foot. The wound wasn't deep, but it bled a little. I couldn't feel Chrissie's pain physically, but emotionally I could feel everything. I wished the nail had gone into *my* foot. I wanted to take her pain away. It caused me pain to see her hurting. If she was hurting, I wanted to hurt beside her. I wanted to share her pain.

Chrissie could easily strike up a conversation and make friends. I was happy to jump in on her new friendships and was always welcomed in. But when junior high rolled around, I faced a new challenge. We had different class schedules, which meant we were in different parts of the campus. Navigating new hallways and new friendships without her by my side felt overwhelming. I had leaned on her for so long that I didn't know how to navigate life on my own. Junior high was disorienting enough on its own. I felt awkward in my body and out of place at our new school. Now I didn't have Chrissie to lean on. When I walked down the hall and heard a group of students laughing, I was certain they were making fun of me. The world felt scary, and I felt alone. I didn't know who I was without my other half.

Then things got even more difficult when Chrissie was put into honors classes. Honors classes were for students who exceled in academics. Honors students got to do special activities to further their education and help them achieve even more, such as attending a local ballet or symphony performance. I was not in honors classes. I didn't get straight A's like Chrissie. I felt small and unseen. Chrissie always laughed about her honors classes and said they were no big deal. She said the ballet was boring and I wasn't missing anything. But it was hard not to feel left out and less than.

My dad pulled me aside one evening and gently told me, "You are just as smart as Chrissie. You don't need to be in honors classes to prove you're smart. You don't need to be just like Chrissie; you can just be you."

I wanted to be me, but I had no idea who I was.

I continued to compare myself to Chrissie. Even though we were identical twins, she always seemed stronger, braver, smarter, and prettier than me. I wished I could be more like her, which is ironic, considering we were identical twins.

Comparing felt natural—part of my world, part of being a twin. And it wasn't just Chrissie that I compared myself to. I compared myself to the popular girls at school, to the models in my teen magazine, to actresses on TV. *Am I good enough? Am I pretty enough? Am I smart enough?* I was certain that the answer to all those questions was no. And if I wasn't special, I reasoned it was better not to be noticed. It was easier to hide in the shadows than to stand in the sunshine. I didn't want attention on me; I wanted to disappear.

If I didn't need anything, if I didn't want anything, maybe I could slip by under the radar. Maybe people wouldn't notice I wasn't good enough. It was just a few years earlier that I had stopped allowing myself to want the red bowl. Once again, it was easier to just go with the flow. Maybe if other people got what they wanted, if I could make them happy, they would love me. If they loved me, maybe I would feel like I was good enough.

As a child, I wanted to believe that God made me special, but I didn't feel special. I wanted to believe I was enough, but I didn't know how. What does it mean to be unique and precious? I wasn't sure.

Side by Side

Side by side,
Comparing you to me,
Comparing me to you—
Who is better?

Better than what?
What are we comparing?
What ruler are we using?
How will we know?

I'm better today,
But it brings me no rest.
You're better tomorrow—
The game never ends.

I hide myself away;
You wear a mask.
We are near each other
But so far apart.

We constantly guess
And measure and wonder,
Am I good enough?
Will I belong?

No longer side by side,
Now back to back.
Comparison steals
Our affections.

I withhold my heart—
It's too scary to share
The real me
With the perceived you.

If I win, you lose.
If you win, I lose.
When we are compared,
We cannot both win.

What if I love you
The way you are
And you love me too
The way I am—

Side by side?
You be just you;
I'll be just me;
And we will both win—

Both of us together:
Honest,
Present,
Wholehearted.

Finally, our truest selves.
We see with new eyes—
We are different and alike.
We are best when we are ourselves.

chapter three

THE LADDER

Throughout junior high and into high school, I did my best to make other people happy so they would love me, but it wasn't working. Instead of feeling loved, I felt hollow and dissatisfied.

Why can't I have what I want? I thought. I blamed other people for my emptiness, unaware that I was creating my own dysfunctional dynamic. By the time I entered college, my frustration had turned to bitterness and eventually to an undercurrent of depression. I was trying hard to control everyone and everything, but I felt completely out of control.

I saw this dynamic play out as I began dating. I had some good relationships and some not co-good relationships. The difficult relationships weren't hard because the guys were bad guys, but because we weren't a good fit. I wanted something from them they couldn't give me. I wanted to make them okay so I would be okay. I wanted to please my boyfriends. Instead of wanting to be accepted for who I was, I wanted to be who they wanted me to be.

A healthy relationship is made up of two people who show up, speak up, and have the courage to be who they truly are. It requires whole people who lovingly and honestly engage in—rather than avoid—real life, including the messiness that it inevitably entails.

But as a young woman who had lost touch with who she was, I wasn't capable of showing up and speaking up. So I focused on fixing up instead. I chose young men I could "help." It's a dynamic that played out in extreme ways in one of my relationships in particular. I chose a boyfriend who was in a deep, dark hole. He was in a bad place, and I was determined to help him through the darkness. He was failing classes and had overdue bills, and his apartment was a disaster. I was sure I could save him.

I was walking across my college campus when I saw him for the first time. He was tall with wavy brown hair, olive skin, and a sparkle in his eyes. I was drawn to him, but I pushed the feeling down. I told myself there was no way he'd be interested in me.

A couple of days later, as I stood in line at the campus coffee shop, he walked up behind me. Before I had a chance to feel self-conscious, I turned around and smiled. He smiled back and introduced himself. I was usually quiet around guys, so I couldn't believe how natural this felt. We ended up sipping our coffee together and talking for an hour. He called me that evening, and we watched a movie together. After that, we were a couple. We spent our evenings cuddling on the couch. On weekends, we hiked a nearby trail or relaxed at the beach. After a couple of months, we were already talking about marriage. He seemed to have it all—good looks, good grades, good personality. He was exactly the type of guy I wanted to marry, or so I thought.

Our relationship had started out feeling good, but within a few weeks, I started to see some red flags. I ignored them, excused them, tried to wish them away. But the red flags kept coming. When things took a turn, the relationship deteriorated quickly. He had a dark side. There were times he became harsh and unreasonable, and his temper scared me. At the time, I didn't know he had an addiction, but I could see that his life was spinning out of control. He had unpaid parking tickets and was always running late, and his apartment was an absolute mess. One evening, he almost got in a fistfight with a stranger at a movie theater.

Regardless, I was determined to stay with him. I reminded myself that he was in a deep, dark hole, and I was sure I could help him. I could offer him a ladder of power. A tool to access the deep knowing inside of him in order to find the way forward. I thought maybe I could hold his ladder and help him climb out. So I tried to manage his schedule, remind him about important meetings, and loan him money. I felt certain I was strong enough to fill in the gaps, to make up for what he lacked. I tried to be enough for both of us. I tried to hold his ladder steady, but instead of stepping on the rungs, he stepped on me.

After a fight, he would often surprise me with little gifts, such as a favorite cinnamon roll from a local bakery or a single rose. He had a sweet side, and I tried to focus on that instead of the nagging feeling inside that told me this wasn't right. *Part of being in relationship is being together in the dark places*, I told myself. *Relationships are hard, right? We can figure this out. I can help him.*

But things continued to get only darker and messier. The good was good, but the bad was terrible. When most people would have run, I stayed. I was committed, even if it meant jumping into that deep, dark hole with him. I would not cut and run. I would hold his ladder for him. It was the loving, selfless thing to do.

So I did. But the hole was much deeper than I expected, and I was losing myself in his darkness. He hurt me over and over. His angry outbursts and irresponsibility left me wounded and confused. Despite my efforts, now we were both stuck at the bottom of the hole.

Why does he keep stepping on me? I wondered. *Doesn't he see the sturdy ladder I'm holding for him?*

Things finally came to a head late one afternoon when he was getting ready for an important dinner. He realized the sport coat he needed was at a dry cleaning shop that closed in twenty minutes.

"Is it the cleaners on Broad Street?" I asked.

"Yes," he said distractedly.

"Don't worry, babe," I said. I hopped in my car and raced to the cleaners. When I arrived, the teenage girl behind the counter explained that my boyfriend's account had a past due balance of $36. The store required a cash payment before releasing any garments. I didn't have any cash, and there were only nine minutes left before closing.

Why can't he take care of anything?

I ran across the street to an ATM, withdrew $40 from my almost empty bank account, and ran back to the cleaners with no time to spare. The girl behind the counter processed my payment and then delivered the bad news. "We don't have his sport coat," she said.

"Wait, what?" I asked, confused and out of breath. "What do you mean?"

"We don't have any garments under his name," she repeated. "I'm required to collect on overdue accounts, but yeah, we don't have his coat."

I stormed outside and called my boyfriend. "Your coat is at the cleaners on Broad Street, right?" I yelled.

"Oh, sorry, babe!" he said. "It's actually at the cleaners on Main Street."

Fury coursed through my veins. I was so tired of this. So very tired and angry. This type of chaos was happening almost every day. Life had become one crisis after another, and I was tired of bailing him out.

I was trying to help him, but he had stepped on me one time too many. I was done. We argued late into the night. After hours of negotiating and tears, we broke up. No matter how hard I tried to help him climb out of the mess he was in, it never worked. I wanted out.

Once it was over, I was sad, but also relieved. I had stayed with him for almost two years of chaos and drama, and I was exhausted. I had been so busy trying to save him that I didn't realize how much of myself I'd lost along the way. In the days and weeks that followed, life began to feel brighter and lighter. I had more energy to focus on my own life. *Why was I so determined to hold his ladder when I had my own ladder to climb?*

I started spending time with my girlfriends again, something I loved but had stopped doing while we were dating. He hated country music, and so after we broke up, I started listening to country music—to this day I still love country music. I redid my bedroom, painting the walls a bright yellow and covering the bed with a vintage cream cover. I focused renewed energy on my job, which I had been neglecting. I also spent more time hanging out with my closest friends.

Eventually, I heard through mutual friends that my ex was doing better. Now that I was out of his life, he was taking responsibility for himself and getting the help he needed. He had found his ladder. It was a long time before I realized that my efforts to help him—to hold his ladder—were actually hindrances. How could he take responsibility for his life when I was so determined to take responsibility for him? He couldn't get to his ladder because I was blocking it. The more I tried to help, the worse things became. He didn't need me to hold his ladder; he could climb it on his own. Or not. But either way, it was never my ladder to begin with.

I wish I could say that was the last time I tried to hold someone else's ladder, but it wasn't. In fact, it's a lesson I'm still learning, slowly but surely. I have my own ladder to climb—a sturdy and stable ladder that will take me where I need to go. We all have our own ladders, the rungs we need to climb to grow and move forward in life. Every rung requires bravery. I can cheer for a friend or my sister or my husband. I can encourage my kids as they go higher, rung by rung. When someone I love is struggling, I can speak words of love and truth. I can remind them they are capable and brave.

But I cannot hold their ladder—and they cannot hold mine. When I tried to hold my boyfriend's ladder, not only was I not climbing my own ladder, but I was getting in his way. We each have our own ladder to climb. We each have a deep knowing inside us to guide us as we make our way through life. It's a journey each of us must make on our own. And most importantly, I'm learning we each have the power to do it.

My Ladder

I have a ladder that's all my own, and you have one as well.

My ladder connects every particle of my body to every piece of my soul. It's as real as it is invisible.

My ladder is completely unique to me, just as yours is unique to you.

My ladder is sturdy and stable.

All ladders are.

My ladder is made up of hearty fibers bound together by my God-given wisdom and power.

My ladder is stabilized by love, strengthened by honesty, and restored by forgiveness.

My ladder is infused with hope and possibility.

When I ignore my thoughts and deny my feelings, I lose hold of my ladder.

My ladder is always within reach, just like your ladder is within reach.

I am safer on my ladder.

Stepping off solid ground and onto my ladder can be terrifying.

But I am learning that my ladder is sturdy and stable.

All ladders are.

By holding tightly to my ladder, I climb higher and grow into my truest self.

My truest self is the beautiful, worthy person God created me to be.

chapter four

MEETING STEVE

I wanted to have fun. I was tired of arguing and fixing and
pretending. I was tired of the ups and downs, tired of apology
after apology. I wanted easy. I wanted freedom. I wanted to live
in the moment and enjoy myself. No more chaos, no more drama.

So when my roommate invited me to join her and her
boyfriend—and her boyfriend's roommate, Steve—in taking
swing dance class, I was all in. It was *not* a setup, just a dance
class. There were no expectations, and it sounded easy and fun.
I was not much of a dancer, but I figured I could learn. I wanted
to be brave and stretch myself. So, instead of playing it safe like I
used to do, I decided to go for it.

I had met Steve before. He had come over to help my five
roommates and me move into the three-bedroom house we were
sharing in Fullerton, California. We were all Biola University
graduates trying to find jobs so we could repay our school loans.
It was a sweet time in my life—living with those amazing girls,
navigating boyfriends, decorating our cute home, hosting parties, and staying up late talking. There were often lots of people
around. Steve and I were getting to know each other as part of a
larger group of friends.

He's just a dance partner, and I'm just having fun, I reminded myself as this cute guy wearing Gap khakis and stylish glasses took my hand and led me onto the dance floor. When he spun me around, I felt light and happy and free. I loved holding hands with him while we moved in rhythm to the beat. After class, we often stayed up late talking.

I do not have feelings for Steve, I assured myself. *He's a nice guy and we connect, but there's nothing more. We're just friends.*

Week after week, we met up and drove together to dance class. We talked, laughed, and debated various subjects. Sometimes after dance class, we'd go out for dessert and talk. When we got back to my house, he'd stick around. One evening, we read poetry together, going through each poem line by line and discussing its meaning. Steve had studied literature and the classics. I loved hearing his thoughts and spending time with him, but I kept telling myself I had no feelings for him.

Why do I spend so much time with this guy? I wondered, as I continued to deny any attraction to him. "You and Steve would make a cute couple," my roommates said. Over and over, I assured them we were only friends, nothing more. Even as I assured them —and myself—that I did not have feelings for Steve, I kept spending time with him. And when we were together, I lingered. I didn't want it to end. He lingered too.

When the swing dance class ended, we took another dance class, and then another. As we learned the steps in class, we danced with different partners. We moved around the room in two large circles—the men on the outside, the women on the inside. We rotated until every man had danced with every woman, but Steve was officially *my* dance partner. We arrived together; we left together; we started each class dancing together; and when given the option, we always chose to dance with each other. We were committed partners inside our dance class, but nothing more than friends outside it.

After several weeks of dancing together, the classes ended. "I hope he doesn't ask me out on a date," I told my roommates. "I don't have feelings for him. I just want to have fun."

A couple of nights after our final dance class, the phone rang. It was Steve asking me to go out to dinner and see a movie. *Crap!* Caught off guard and with no good excuse, I said yes. He wanted to take me to The Old Spaghetti Factory and then to see the movie *Hope Floats*. He knew the restaurant was my favorite, and he knew I wanted to see that movie. He's a smart guy. We went out and had a great time. Then we went out again, and again. So we were kind of dating, but I was still unsure of how I felt about him.

One evening, after a fun gathering with lots of friends, we hung out late into the night talking and laughing. That was the evening Steve told me he had feelings for me. He wanted to be more than friends. I didn't know what to say. Here's this guy who was amazing. He was cute; he had style; he had insights he was willing to share; and we definitely had a connection. He seemed to be so many things my ex-boyfriend wasn't, so many things I wanted in a boyfriend and maybe someday a husband. As we sat there on the couch, I knew I didn't want to hurt him. I also knew I wanted to continue hanging out with him. But I still wasn't completely sure how I felt about him.

I ended up telling him I wanted to be careful with him. It was vague and kind, and it seemed to satisfy him. We talked awhile longer and then hugged good night. When we hung out together the next day, Steve told me he had initially felt happy about our conversation but had later realized I hadn't reciprocated his feelings. He asked me directly, "Do you have feelings for me?"

There was a pause—one that lasted a little too long. I wasn't sure what to say. I wanted to be honest, but I didn't want to hurt him. I wasn't ready to commit to a future with him, but I also didn't want to end our friendship. I was confused. He was so confused. I thought maybe I felt fearful since things had ended so badly with my previous relationship. Thankfully, Steve was willing to endure some uncertainty.

A couple of weeks later, Steve told me that a childhood friend—who lived four hours away—was getting married, and they planned to have swing dancing at the reception.

"Will you join me?" he asked. "After all, we're officially dance partners." It sounded like fun and I wanted to go, but there was one big problem (in addition to my uncertainty about my feelings). My parents were very conservative, and there was no way I could go out of town with a guy before they met him. "You'll have to meet my parents first," I said.

Two days later, we met my parents for pizza. We sat in a booth with red vinyl seats while they asked him questions and got to know him. The conversation was easy and light. We laughed, joked, and enjoyed each other. Of course, they loved him.

"This is a great guy," my parents said. "Date him!"

"I'm not sure I have feelings for him," I said. But I was beginning to think that maybe, just maybe, there was something there. A little spark.

My parents approved, and Steve and I made plans to travel to the wedding together. After all, we were official dance partners.

The weekend of the wedding, Steve picked me up and loaded my suitcase into the trunk of his car. As I buckled myself in, I realized I felt excited. A road trip! An adventure! This was going to be fun!

I must feel something for him, I thought. *Why else would I be so excited?*

Long car rides can be awkward or easy. Our conversation was easy, and it was also deep and honest. We were connecting in a new way. We asked each other good questions and listened to each other. We talked about school, roommates, hobbies, and our most embarrassing moments. Our hearts were getting to know each other.

Since I wasn't sure of my feelings for Steve, I didn't feel pressured to impress him or to pretend to be someone I was not. I told him about my ex-boyfriend—how I was afraid of his bad temper, how we had fought, and about my frustrations with all of the chaos. He listened and gave me good insights. Something in my heart shifted. I was beginning to trust Steve.

When we arrived at Steve's parents' house, I met his mom and dad and got settled in the guest room. That afternoon, the battery in Steve's car died, and we decided to try push-starting it. Despite everything my dad had taught me about cars, I had never "popped the clutch" before. I was assigned to the driver's seat. While Steve and his dad pushed the car, my job was to depress the clutch and then release it as soon as the car had a little speed. Over and over, they pushed the car and I popped the clutch, but the car wouldn't start. It was 100 degrees outside, and both Steve and his dad were hot, tired, and frustrated.

"Is the car even *on*?" I heard Steve's dad yell.

Oh my gosh! I had no idea the ignition was supposed to be on! It made perfect sense that the car wouldn't start unless the ignition was on, but I was new at this. I discreetly turned the key in the ignition and leaned my head out the window. "Hey, guys, let's give it one more try." They pushed the car; I popped the clutch;

and the car magically started! Finally we had the necessary spark to ignite the engine and set the car in motion.

That evening, Steve and I attended the wedding and then the reception—which was outdoors with lovely table settings and fresh flowers. We found our seats at a table with his close-knit group of high school friends. These were the guys he had hung out with every day growing up. These were the people who knew him better than anyone else. They were welcoming and fun, and, most importantly, they obviously loved him. When they teased him, he laughed easily at himself. It was clear that these guys were close and that they cared about each other. There was a deep bond between them, and I felt honored to get a peek inside their friendship. Seeing the way Steve's close friends loved him shifted something in my heart again.

Oh my gosh, this guy is amazing!

I had convinced myself that I didn't have feelings for Steve, but once I experienced him in this new context and saw how much his friends loved and admired him, my feelings changed. That evening was the spark that ignited my heart and set our relationship in motion.

There is no denying it, I thought. *I like this guy.*

As Steve and I began the drive home, we continued our easy conversation. I couldn't believe how differently I felt. Instead of feeling uncertain, I felt peaceful. My questions were being paired with answers. I knew Steve in a new way. I had been unsure of my feelings when we began our journey to Fresno, but on our return trip, I knew I wanted to date him. I decided to be brave and tell Steve I had feelings for him. He smiled, grateful to put an end to the uncertainty. I saw him exhale. After that, we started dating. Now we weren't just official dance partners; we were officially a couple.

Magic

Magic is how somehow our souls found each other.

Magic is the way our hearts stretch to hold an impossibly
   big love.

Magic is a hug that makes the pain go away.

Magic is the way we light up when we see each other.

Magic is how your hand fits perfectly in mine.

Magic is seeing beauty grow where pain was planted.

Magic is stepping into the unknown

And finding ourselves right where we are meant to be.

Magic is the unshakable love we share.

Magic is knowing you are my answered prayer.

Some don't believe in magic.

But when I look around, I see that

Magic happens every day.

It's happening to me.

chapter five

WE GOT ENGAGED!

S teve and I were a couple for about a year before we got married. Once we started dating, I was fairly certain he would one day be my husband, but we didn't talk about marriage. I had made that mistake with my last boyfriend. Before we were even engaged, my ex and I had picked out names for our kids, chosen household appliances, and done all kinds of other long-term planning. Talk about putting the cart before the horse! When we broke up, it was messy. Breakups are always messy, but our lives, dreams, and even our possessions were so tangled up together that there was a lot that had to be unraveled.

With Steve, I wanted to do things differently. I told him if he wanted to talk about marriage, we should start with a ring. Until then, we would just relax and have fun getting to know each other. He seemed fine with that plan. He didn't want to rush things. He told me he wouldn't say, "I love you," until he had a ring in his hand. He told me how seriously he took those words. He wanted me to know that when he said them, he would be ready to spend the rest of his life with me.

So we relaxed. We had a lot of fun just living in the moment and enjoying each other. Our evenings were often spent making grilled cheese sandwiches, watching a movie with my roommates and their boyfriends, or taking an evening stroll to the nearby Starbucks. The more time I spent with Steve, the more confident I felt about spending my life with him. He loved to have fun. He loved to laugh and talk and be with other people. He loved to be silly and try new things. I felt increasingly convinced that he was the man for me.

We had been dating for about eight months when Steve told me he wanted to take me out for a special dinner at a restaurant near his apartment. That was odd because Steve lived about thirty minutes south of me. *Why would he want to drive all the way north to pick me up, only to turn around and drive all the way back south for dinner?* I had a feeling he was planning something, so I wore a nice dress and heels. I spent time getting my hair just right. Before he arrived, I put on another layer of lipstick. *What if this night turns out to be the night?*

When he arrived on my front porch looking a little nervous and wearing new slacks, I got that funny feeling again. He was so handsome, and that smile was so kissable. His kind eyes held the promise of good things. When he suggested we go for a walk on the pier in Laguna Beach before dinner, I had that funny feeling once more. My heart was beating fast. I was trying to act normal, and he was trying to act normal, but the evening felt anything but normal!

We drove thirty minutes south, holding hands and making small talk. We were lucky to find a parking spot near the pier, and as we got out of the car, he bent down to pull up his socks. We walked a few steps, and he bent down again to adjust his socks.

What's with the socks? Why is he acting so weird?

We walked toward one side of the pier and stood together for a few moments looking out at the crashing waves below.

The evening was cool, and the ocean breeze gave me a little shiver. I was wishing I had brought a sweater when Steve leaned in close and whispered, "I love you."

His words sparked through me like an electric current. I knew he loved me, but when he finally said it, I felt jolted by the power of those three words. I could feel the charged energy between us, and I knew something big was about to happen.

Oh my gosh! This is it!

Before my mind could process exactly what was happening, Steve was on one knee, pulling a small box out of his sock. When he opened the box, I saw a gorgeous, vintage diamond ring. It was a platinum band with a round diamond in the center and smaller diamonds on each side. The sides of the band were etched with scrolling detail. It was simple and stunning.

He was saying something, but his words barely registered. I took the ring out of the box and slipped it on my left hand. I can't remember if I answered his proposal with a "Yes!" or if I was so focused on the ring I neglected to give him a definitive answer. But he knew. He knew by my huge smile and my arms wrapped tightly around his neck. I loved him. I wanted to spend my life with him. I wanted to have a family with him. I'd never been so sure about anything in my life. There was no doubt in my mind that he was the one for me.

As we were hugging, I felt Steve rotate his arm as if he were looking at his watch.

"Do you have somewhere else to be?" I asked, laughing.

"Yep," he said with a smile. "We have dinner reservations, and I don't want to be late."

Hand in hand, we walked back to the car. I could feel the ocean breeze, but I no longer felt cold. I had Steve's "I love you" wrapped around me like a warm blanket.

He opened the car door for me and then walked around to his side of the car. As we drove to the restaurant, I kept staring at the ring on my finger. I loved it. I loved that it was vintage. I loved the way it sparkled. I loved Steve.

The restaurant was just around the corner. He had chosen Italian food, my favorite. As Steve pulled into the parking lot, I saw the name on the side of the building. Our little restaurant near the ocean was called "Ti Amo." I didn't know Italian, but I had taken Spanish in high school. *Ti amo* meant "I love you." It was perfect! Steve had finally said those three words to me, so of course the restaurant should reflect his proclamation of love.

I wanted him to say those words again. Before we got out of the car, I leaned over and said, "I love you." It felt good. It felt right.

"I love you too," he said. I looked at the ring again, soaking up his words. Nobody knew love like ours. We had something special. We were meant to be together. We had this figured out.

The restaurant was cozy, with twinkling lights and beautifully set tables. This was much fancier than our usual fish tacos or In-N-Out burgers. The hostess greeted us with a smile. "Good evening," she said. "Do you have reservations?"

"We just got *engaged!*" I blurted out a little too loudly. It wasn't the answer to her question, but I was dying to share the news with anyone who would listen.

She smiled back at us, sharing in our joy for a moment, and then led us to a table for two toward the back. After we ordered, I split my time between staring at my ring and saying "I love you" to Steve. I felt seen; I felt loved. Surely this was my missing piece, just what I needed to feel complete and whole. I had always been a twin, but Chrissie and I were grown now and leading separate lives. She would always be my sister, but I needed a new partner to walk through life with me. I needed someone new to lean on. It was a perfect night, and I felt certain that Steve and I were a perfect couple.

Come Over

Come over.
Settle in.
Sit down.
Snuggle up.

Let yourself relax.
Let yourself enjoy.
Let yourself let go.
Let yourself be loved.

Make friends.
Make music.
Make messes.
Make memories.

With open hearts,
With honesty,
Without judgment,
With your hand in mine.

Let's dream.
Let's explore.
Let's learn.
Let's be brave.

Today holds newness.
Today holds adventure.
Today holds beauty.
Today holds hope.

We are us.
We are you and me.
We are each other.
We are family.

Slow down.
Breathe deeply.
Be quiet.
Let your heart speak.

Listen closely.
Feel your feelings.
Think outside the box.
See with new eyes.

Forgive.
Forget.
Let your heart
Be free.

All is right.
All is known.
All is safe.
All is well.

No shame,
No fear,
No hiding,
No worry.

You are precious.
You are seen.
You are loved.
You are where you are meant to be.

Be grateful.
Be curious.
Be gentle.
Be you—

One of a kind.
Together we're better.
Three words ("I love you")
Forever, for always.

chapter six

FOREVER PROMISES

I had been planning my dream wedding for years before Steve and I met. During college, I worked part-time as a wedding coordinator, and I had collected bits of inspiration from every wedding I coordinated. Once Steve and I were engaged, I was ready to get to work carrying out my own beautiful wedding. There was just one small problem. We had a painfully small budget of $2,000, and it had to cover the flowers, the photographer, the cake, my dress—everything. Our budget was much smaller than I had hoped for, but it was all we had. I felt my heart deflate as I began crossing ideas off my list. They were simply too expensive. But sometimes a small budget can inspire creativity—and creativity almost always leads to beauty.

I asked my roommates to buy flowers wholesale so they could assemble the bouquets and boutonnieres within our tight budget. The flowers turned out amazing! It was so meaningful to have my dear friends using their time and creativity to make our day beautiful. We asked a friend who was an amateur photographer to shoot our wedding pictures, and she did an outstanding job. Another friend who is a professional photographer brought his camera to the wedding and took some incredible shots throughout the ceremony and reception at no charge. I cherish these images.

Instead of a big fancy cake, we served cheesecake with a variety of toppings—caramel, Oreo cookie crumbles, chocolate sauce. My mom collected vintage teapots, and we potted flowers in each one for the reception table centerpieces.

One of the most cherished parts of my wedding was being able to wear my mother's wedding dress, which my grandmother had sewn for her thirty years before. My mom cut off the sleeves and added lace to the bottom of the dress. It fit perfectly, and I loved wearing this family heirloom. Steve and I didn't need to spend much money on our wedding to make it beautiful. With $2,000, we created a wedding that truly reflected who we were.

Our wedding day came quickly. Just five months after our engagement, my dad offered me his arm; the wedding march music filled the church; and the double doors to the sanctuary opened wide. We walked slowly down the aisle, making eye contact with friends and family as we moved toward the front of the church. With each step, I moved closer to Steve and farther away from my old life. I felt confident and excited. We were a perfect match. We would conquer any trials that came our way. I left behind the life I knew and walked through a new doorway to a new life. I had no idea what might lie on the other side of the doorway, but I pushed forward, my heart full of anticipation.

We were in love. We said our vows with hearts full of hope. We made forever promises. We sealed those promises with a kiss in front of a church full of people. We were married!

Remind Me

Take my hand and
Remind me we belong together.

When gray clouds gather,
Remind me of warmer weather.

If tears fall,
Remind me there is joy to be found.
When knees tremble,
Remind me I'm on solid ground.

If we are apart,
Remind me we'll make our way back.
When I feel empty,
Remind me there's nothing I lack.

If I am serious,
Remind me to be wild and free.
When I look far ahead,
Remind me this moment is key.

If I am angry,
Remind me it's okay to shout.
When I am happy,
Remind me this is what life's about.

If I am tired,
Remind me to rest and sleep more.
When I am confused,
Remind me to search and explore.

If I am lost in questions,
Remind me I don't have to know.
When I am stretched,

Remind me it's how I will grow.

When I fail,
Remind me I can always restart.
If I am lost,
Remind me to look to my heart.

When you forget, don't worry—
I'll remind you that
We are side by side on this journey,
Whatever may be.

chapter seven

NEWLYWEDS

We celebrated our wedding with friends and then drove away from the reception in a forest green vintage Woody. As we drove down the street, Steve still in his tux, me in my gown and veil, I looked at the people in the cars around us. Did they know how amazing today was? Could they tell by looking at us that everything was beginning anew? We were in love and starting our lives together. My heart was exploding with happiness and anticipation.

We spent our first night at a nearby bed-and-breakfast. The room was a splurge, and it had a huge king-sized bed and a giant Roman tub. We looked at each other with stars in our eyes. I loved Steve, and he loved me. Our whole lives were in front of us.

Early the next morning, we woke up groggy from our wedding day and all the excitement surrounding it. Our breakfast was delivered at 5 a.m., a basket right outside our door filled with freshly baked muffins, vanilla yogurt, and ripe berries. It came early because we had a plane to catch—we were going to Hawaii!

Hawaii was nowhere in our meager budget. We had planned to stay close by, keeping our honeymoon simple and affordable. So when a dear friend gifted us with a dream-come-true honeymoon trip, we were both stunned and thrilled. We were going to be in a condo on the beach! For a whole week!

We nibbled on our breakfast while we packed our bags, and then we headed to the airport before the sun was up. We had every reason to be in high spirits, but instead we were tired and grumpy on the flight and stressed as we picked up our rental car to drive to the condo.

Isn't this supposed to be perfect? I thought as I looked out at the gorgeous island around me.

That first honeymoon day wasn't what I thought it would be, but I chalked it up to being tired. So much had happened in the last forty-eight hours—of course we were exhausted. But our second morning in Hawaii, I woke up with a heaviness in my heart. Fear wrapped its cold tendrils around me, and I felt like I was choking. I looked over at Steve next to me in bed and winced.

What have I done?

I didn't have a moment of doubt while we were dating or engaged. During our wedding planning, I was so sure he was the one for me. Now we had been married for forty-eight hours, and I was beginning to question everything.

Do I even love him? I've known this man for less than two years, and I've committed to spending the rest of my life with him? What if marriage is harder than we expected? What if we don't have everything figured out?

I felt sick. Like I might throw up. Like I wanted to run far away.

As Steve stirred, I closed my eyes and pretended to be asleep. My body was motionless, but fear was pounding through my veins.

I'm not ready for marriage.

"Good morning," Steve said with a smile and kissed my forehead. "How's my wife?"

I smiled back at him, my heart sinking in my chest. It would crush him when I told him how I was feeling.

"Let's go get some breakfast," he said. *Poor guy*, I thought. *He's so happy.*

Over breakfast, I looked at Steve, my voice shaking, and said, "I need to tell you something."

"Okay, what's up?" he said, not a hint of worry in his voice.

"I . . . I . . . I don't think I love you," I said, my eyes starting to fill with tears. "I think I've made a huge mistake."

He smiled wide and laughed. "Sweetheart, I think you're freaking out a little. It's all okay. Let's just relax. We can go snorkeling and hang out on the beach. You can decide later if you love me or not."

Huh, he didn't take that as hard as I thought he would. I exhaled. *All right, I'll go with the flow. Maybe I am just freaking out.*

We snorkeled, ate amazing food, lay in the sand, watched the sunset, and loved our time in Hawaii. The fear melted away, and I remembered how much I really did love Steve. I hadn't made a mistake marrying him. But I was right about one thing: Marriage was going to be much harder than we expected. We definitely did not have everything figured out.

Our first two years of marriage were wonderful. We felt solid. Of course, we hadn't known what to expect, but we were well matched. Steve finished grad school, preparing to be a pastor, while I taught children with special needs at a nearby public school. We were young and in love. Our life together was busy but uncomplicated. We decorated our apartment together. Steve did the laundry, and I made dinner. Neither of us liked cleaning the bathroom, but we made it work. We were a family now, he and I, and we were looking forward to having children. Together, we were learning how to be married, how to live life together, how to be us. When we looked at the horizon, all we saw was hope and good things ahead.

Together

What is together?
Two hearts known,
Two hearts sewn,
Loving each other
Despite distance,
Despite time.
Two of a kind.

What is apart?
Playing it safe,
Two hearts in place,
Cautious and careful,
Tiptoeing,
Near but not known,
On our own.

What binds us?
Fully you, fully me,
Completely we.
Honest and true,
Whatever comes.
Side by side forever,
Two hearts together.

chapter eight

SOUL CONNECTION

While Steve and I were engaged, I began substitute teaching in our local school district. After working in both general education and special education classrooms, I was increasingly drawn toward special education. I felt a strong connection with the students. For months, I moved around the district, substitute teaching at different schools and working with students from preschool through high school.

Once I got to know the teachers and the different campuses, I began to get requests from teachers who wanted me to cover their classrooms while they were out. Each day was different, and while I loved the variety, I longed for routine. I was surprised and thrilled when I was offered the opportunity to fill in as a long-term substitute for a combined class of third, fourth, and fifth graders who had special needs. I had subbed for the teacher many times, and I loved this class. The kids were energetic and engaged, and the instructional aides were kind and insightful. I jumped at the chance to spend a few weeks with these students.

A few weeks turned into a month; a month turned into two months. Then I was offered a full-time position as the permanent teacher for this class. There were students in wheelchairs, students with tracheotomy tubes (breathing tubes), students who were fed directly into the stomach through a gastrostomy tube, students who were nonverbal, and students with autism. Working with them, I began to see past their disabilities. They were typical kids trapped inside bodies that would not cooperate.

Every morning, I met the buses at the front of the school at 8:30 a.m., and every afternoon my students boarded the buses at 2:40 p.m. to head home. In between, we were getting to know each other, learning, growing, and connecting. Each student had unique challenges, although most of them were nonverbal. I was beginning to understand their preferences and personalities. We connected through music and singing songs. We read books and played bingo. We worked on feeding and self-help skills, such as brushing teeth and putting books away. We practiced writing their names and used special computer games. We created art by painting and gluing and coloring.

We were working together physically and mentally, forging a deeper bond. I felt like I knew them inside and out. I was surprised to realize one day that, just as I was getting to know their souls, they were getting to know mine. I could see their faces light up when they saw me outside the bus in the morning They engaged wholeheartedly in our classroom activities—from the morning calendar circle to afternoon bingo. A positive energy grew between us that felt natural and easy. We developed routines with each other, and we were able to communicate—often without words.

After teaching for a couple of years, I found a rhythm for planning lessons and creative activities to draw out the students. I felt like maybe I was getting this whole teaching thing down at last. Now I was six months pregnant. I spent my days working with my amazing students and my weekends preparing for the arrival of our soon-to-be-born baby.

There was a little boy in my class named Trent who was non-verbal, shy, and very smart. I didn't want to pick favorites, but Trent had a gentleness and determination about him that I loved. Week by week, he was growing and learning new things. I enjoyed working with him and challenging him to try new things. One day after school, his mother pulled me aside to talk.

"I want to tell you something about Trent," she said, "but I'm not sure how it will make you feel."

"Okay," I said tentatively. She had my full attention.

"Trent has a sixth sense," she said. She paused and waited for my reaction.

"I am not sure what you mean," I replied. "What is a sixth sense?"

"Well, he can read minds," she said. "I know it sounds crazy, and maybe you won't believe me, but it's true. Trent can read minds."

"Okay," I said hesitatingly, trying to take in this news. It sounded strange, but somehow her statement didn't shock me. I felt a strong connection to each student, even though most were nonverbal. Perhaps there was a deeper form of communication that was taking place. Although I had never experienced anything like this before, I decided to keep an open mind.

"I'll work with him tomorrow and let you know if I experience anything that looks like mind reading," I promised.

Some of the nonverbal children in my class typed on a computer keyboard to communicate. Trent's mother had explained that when a person was sitting close to Trent while he was typing, he could read that person's thoughts.

The next day, I decided to ask Trent to read my mind while he was typing. After we took attendance and did our lunch count and our daily calendar activities, I sat down with Trent at the computer.

I was six months pregnant with our first baby, and although Steve and I had chosen a name, we had not told anyone else what it was. I had not even told Chrissie, my identical twin. Steve and I wanted to keep the name a secret until our baby was born.

"Good morning, Trent," I typed, watching the letters appear on the computer screen.

"Good morning," he typed in response.

"How did you sleep last night?" I typed.

"Fine," he answered back on the screen.

Okay, time to explore this mind-reading business, I thought. *What is something Trent couldn't possibly know?*

That's when I decided to ask him our baby's name. It was a perfect question, because there was no way he could know.

"What are we going to name my baby?" I typed.

Trent slowly typed out the words, "David Stephen Leonard."

Impossible! I was so stunned that I couldn't breathe.

I sat still for a few moments, staring at the computer screen.

How could Trent know the baby's name? We haven't told anyone!

"What did I have for breakfast this morning?" I tapped out on the keyboard.

"Banana milkshake," he typed in response.

He was right, and I felt panicky and scared. *He knows my baby's name? He knows what I had for breakfast? It doesn't make sense! How can this be?*

I stood up and told my aides I'd be back in just a moment. I stepped into the hallway to catch my breath.

What in the world just happened? Could someone have told him the baby's name? Did I let it slip out accidentally? I knew those were not possibilities. Trent could not have known my baby's name. He couldn't have known I had a banana milkshake for breakfast.

I hadn't told him. I hadn't told anyone. There was no other explanation—he had read my mind! The rest of the day was a blur as I tried to absorb this new experience.

I went home that afternoon eager to tell Steve about the day's events. When he came home from work, I quickly laid out all the details of my typed conversation with Trent. I explained how Trent not only knew I had a banana milkshake for breakfast, but he also knew *our baby's name.* Steve listened closely, as fascinated by the interaction as I was.

"How can this be?" I asked.

Steve was a pastor, and I was hoping he would have a spiritual explanation or at least some insights to share, but he was just as baffled as I was. Together, we processed and talked and tried to make sense of something that didn't make sense.

Although initially shocked and a little fearful, when I stepped back from the situation a bit, I realized I wasn't really scared. Trent was a sweet and smart nine-year-old boy. Steve and I concluded there must be a soul connection happening—something beyond the physical. Human beings are both body and soul—two parts that make a whole person. Trent must be more in touch with this soul connection than most people. It made sense to me that we were connected by an unseen force, one that he could access better than I could.

I had felt this kind of deep soul connection before. My connection with Chrissie was strong, probably the strongest connection I felt with anyone on earth. It was like our hearts knew each other. It was a connection that went well beyond words, the kind of bond an expectant mother has with her unborn child. Or the connection we have with a friend that prompts us to call, only to find out she really needed words of encouragement *at that very moment.* It is a connection of deep knowing that is cultivated over time.

It was difficult to explain, but I began to realize what I was experiencing with Trent was familiar—I had experienced that kind of connection before. What I didn't know was that in just a few short months, I would have the opportunity to experience it again—this time with my own son with special needs.

Today Holds Beauty

Today holds beauty.

Beauty is ours to find.

Find a moment for quiet.

Quiet makes room for wonder.

Wonder nurtures imagination.

Imagination becomes inspiration.

Inspiration moves the heart.

Heart and hands work together.

Together we create—

Create with bravery.

Bravery helps us stretch and grow—

Grow and change and become,

Become who we were made to be.

Be open to new things,

Things that push us forward—

Forward step by step.

Step into today.

Today holds beauty.

chapter nine

BECOMING A MOTHER

Tension filled the silent labor and delivery room. Much like the oppressive humidity of a hot summer day, the air was thick with fear. I sat up in bed, my back supported by pillows. I was surrounded by five doctors, a nurse, Steve, and my twin sister, all of whom were ready to spring into action the minute our baby was born.

We all knew something was wrong. It's why the doctors had decided to induce labor two weeks early. It's why Steve and I had met with a perinatologist the day before. She had confirmed that our baby was small—too small.

"Expect problems," she told us.

Expect problems. I had heard those words before. I knew they were common English words, and yet my brain couldn't make sense of them.

"What kind of problems?" I asked, my voice trembling. I was fighting the tears but failing in my efforts to hold them back.

"The baby could have a genetic disorder," she said, "or a fatal condition."

Twenty-four hours later, I was in the delivery room, and a nurse was gently encouraging me, "One more really good push."

I pushed with all my might. I pushed past the stifling silence in the room. I pushed past the fear. I pushed through to bring my baby into the world. I pushed forward into the unknown. And as I pushed, I left behind the life I knew. Once again, I was walking through a new doorway. I had no idea what was on the other side, but I pushed ahead with all my might.

Our sweet baby David came into the world silently. The doctors whispered and moved quickly behind me as they cleaned him, weighed him, measured him, and evaluated him. After what felt like an eternity, Steve brought him to my bedside and placed him in my arms.

I cradled my precious, four-pound baby, taking in every part of him. I touched his soft, full head of hair and stroked his beautiful pale skin. I held his small hand in mine, his left hand with only two fingers. I let my eyes take in the sweetest face I had ever seen.

"Here you are," I whispered. "You are small, but you are strong. You must fight harder than most. Life will not be easy for you."

"Expect problems," the perinatologist had said.

I hadn't expected to have a baby with a deformity. I hadn't expected missing fingers. We'd had a few ultrasounds during my pregnancy, and somehow the doctors had missed David's small hand. No one expected this. No one expected that our little David would face his own Goliath on the day of his birth.

As I cradled my tiny baby, I could feel the world as I knew it slipping away. Just a few days before, we'd had lunch with friends, talking and laughing and dreaming about who this baby would be. I hardly recognized myself in the memory. I had pushed through the doorway into an utterly unfamiliar and painful new life.

In the coming days, grief would crash over me like storm-tossed ocean waves. I grieved the loss of the young woman I had been. I grieved the loss of my carefree life. I feared that pain would now be my constant companion.

I grieved the baby I lost, the one from my imagination who never existed. I grieved for what this sweet baby would never have—a normal life, a normal childhood. I grieved the end of our perfect story.

We had stepped through the doorway and into the unknown. I knew we had begun a difficult journey, but I couldn't yet see the unimaginable beauty that lay ahead.

The first days of David's life were full of beeps and buzzes from various equipment in the neonatal intensive care unit (NICU). But the jangling noises around us were nothing compared to the loud voice in my head that couldn't stop asking why.

Why? Why? Why? Why is this happening to us? Why does our son have a disability?

I pleaded with God to help me make sense of the chaos in my mind. Accomplishing the most basic tasks felt like a heroic feat. Just taking a shower or eating a snack was exhausting. Every moment was filled with more questions.

Holding David close to my chest, I let my thoughts wander. A dark thought crossed my mind. *Maybe David will die and we'll be able to forget this whole thing ever happened.* As soon as that thought came, it was quickly followed by another. *God, please, please don't let my baby die!* I was a mix of conflicting thoughts and emotions. I was broken, on my knees, unable to stand. I had nothing to offer God or anyone else. I was empty, except for the whys that haunted me.

Two days after David's birth, I looked out the hospital window to see a familiar oak tree. Steve and I had passed that tree week after week while attending prenatal classes at the hospital. It stood between two driveways, one driveway entering the hospital and the other exiting the hospital. Its tall, sturdy branches extended high and wide, dense with leaves. Although I had seen it several times, I hadn't really noticed it. But on this day, it took me by surprise. *My whole world has turned upside down. How can that old oak tree still be standing?* Everything around me looked the same, exactly the same, but I was not the same. I did not know myself at all. *Who am I?* I entered the hospital one person, but I would exit the hospital a different person.

We drove by that oak tree every day for weeks while our tiny baby was in the hospital. It stood there, tall and confident, a symbol of the unchanging world around us. I resented that oak tree standing there as if nothing had happened. It stood steady between the way in and the way out, a silent witness to the fact that Steve and I were not the same people who arrived at the hospital the day David was born. Everything had changed.

As I looked out the window, I thought about Trent and what he had taught me—that we human beings are body and soul. There is an unseen force connecting us. We are capable of loving deeply without words. I did not know what David's life would hold. I did not know what abilities or disabilities he would have, but I knew he had a beautiful soul. I knew there was a whole soul inside his precious and broken little body.

At the cellular level, every bit of David's body had a chromosomal abnormality. His body was not the way it was supposed to be. If it were a map, we might say the coordinates were incorrectly labeled. If it were a recipe, we could say it didn't have the correct ingredients in the correct amounts. If it were a computer, we might say there was a typo in the operating system code. By any measure, David's body was broken, imperfect, flawed. His soul, on the other hand, was intact and whole. David was body *and* soul. His soul simply resided in a body that did not cooperate—because it could not cooperate.

I wanted to know David's beautiful soul, and I wanted him to know mine. I thought about the connection I had with Trent. I thought about the connection I had with Chrissie and how she knew me through and through. I hoped that David and I could forge an even deeper connection. After all, he was part of me. I was his mother and he was my son.

If that unchanging oak tree could have talked, maybe it would have steadied our souls with words of assurance and comfort. *Breathe deeply. Hold on to hope. Beautiful things are ahead—a connection deeper than you can imagine.* I wanted to believe that, but I couldn't feel it yet. I was still grieving, still trying to make sense of a world that seemed to make no sense at all.

Weather of the Heart

Lord, send the rain
To wash away
The pain
And sadness
And bring life.

Lord, send the wind
To blow away
The doubts
And uncertainty
And make space.

Lord, send the snow
To cover
The mess
And make it white
And clean.

Lord, send the fog
To narrow
My perspective
And help me be present
And focused.

Lord, send the sun
To warm
My shoulders
And comfort my heart
And soul.

chapter ten

GRIEF AND GIFT

Extreme, soul-breaking grief took me apart. What was, was no longer. What would be, was unknown. I was brought face-to-face with my complete lack of control, my utter lack of understanding. There was no pretending I had it all together, no way to fake anything at all. Grief took away all my defenses and left me exposed and naked.

I was starting a whole new life from scratch. I began again, step by tiny step. *Wake up. Brush teeth. Put on clothes. Eat something.* Every small action required extreme effort because I was learning how to do everything again in the face of the unknown.

I remembered the woman I used to be—the one who was carefree and laughed easily. That's who I was before my son was born with a severe disability, before my baby was born with a hand that had just two fingers, before the world stopped turning. I couldn't imagine I would ever laugh or feel carefree again.

For the first few weeks of David's life, time slowed to a crawl. The minutes dragged on and on—hours felt like days, weeks felt like months, months felt like years. While the rest of the world moved on at normal speed, I felt like I was living multiple lifetimes in slow-motion grief.

Why? Why? Why?

For weeks, that one-word question circled my brain like a broken record spinning round and round.

Why does our baby have a disability? Why is this happening to us? Why, God?

For a while, it seemed like my questions fell into an empty void, echoing back nothing but more questions. *Do I even believe in God? Is God real? Does he love me? Why would God allow this pain?* The questions played in my head on loud and endless repeat. I never got all the answers, but I eventually began to feel a slow and sweet assurance. *Yes, I believe in God. I don't understand what's happening or why, but I believe that the God of the universe loves me. I believe that he loves David.* And yet even this raised more questions.

Then why, God? If you love me, if you love my baby, why?

It was a question I prayed over and over.

Eventually, God spoke to my heart—not with words, not with an answer exactly, but with a soothing calm. *I am giving you a gift,* he whispered. *Just trust me.*

The doctors told us David had Cornelia de Lange syndrome.*

"He'll never walk or talk," they said. "He will be severely retarded."

What was, was no longer. What would be, was unknown. Unknown to me, but not to God.

A gift? This doesn't feel like a gift, but I believe you are God, I whispered. *I'm confused. Nothing makes sense. Help me, God. Help me to see the gift in this pain.*

For the first three weeks of David's life, we went home every evening to our apartment while our baby remained behind in the

---

* For information on Cornelia de Lange syndrome, visit www.cdlsusa.org.

NICU. Parents were not permitted in the unit during the daily shift change—when the day staff left and the night staff arrived. I wanted to be with David twenty-four hours a day while he was in the NICU, but that wasn't an option. We needed to eat. We needed to sleep. We needed to take a break. But leaving him was torture. Every night at 7 p.m., my heart broke as we said good-bye and kissed David's tiny forehead. We walked to our car without our son. Our arms were empty when they should have been full with our baby, a diaper bag, and a car seat.

Every evening, we drove past that big oak tree as we left the hospital. We were strangers in our new lives—strangers to each other and to ourselves. The oak tree was a painful reminder that while it seemed like everything had changed, really *we* were the ones who had changed. At the sight of the oak tree, I felt alone. The world was the same and had moved on without us. The oak tree stood there as if nothing had happened, and yet our lives were turned completely upside down.

Every evening, I prayed the same prayer: *Please, God, comfort my baby when I cannot be there. Hold him and nurture him while he sleeps in his incubator. Give my baby what I cannot give him.*

We moved through the motions of our days in the NICU. We held David, changed his diapers, and practiced feeding him through a tube running through his nose into his stomach. Our two-bedroom apartment was only a couple miles from the hospital. David's room was ready for him, but it had been prepared for a different baby. Inside the dresser drawers were clothes for an eight-pound baby, not a four-pound baby. We didn't have one item of clothing that would fit our tiny David. The car seat needed to be adjusted to the smallest setting, and even then, we'd have to tuck blankets around David to keep him secure. The newborn diapers we had purchased wouldn't fit David for another four months. We were as unprepared materially for the arrival of our new baby as we were emotionally.

One afternoon a few days after David was born, I stepped outside the NICU and sat in the lobby with our checkbook and a folder full of bills. Even in a crisis, real life demands to be lived. Bills had to be paid. Cars needed gas. Dishes had to be washed.

This is so strange, I thought. *My baby was born with a severe medical condition and two fingers on his left hand. Who cares about the gas bill?*

It felt surreal to do normal, everyday tasks when our world had crumbled around us. As I wrote the first check and tucked it inside an envelope, our friends Josh and Maggie walked into the lobby. In the early years of our marriage, they had been our upstairs neighbors, worked in ministry with us, and were among our closest friends. They quietly joined me on the uncomfortable lobby couch. They offered no words, just a compassionate and tender silence. I set the bills aside, buried my head in my hands, and began to sob. The tears came from a bottomless well of grief, and I wondered if I would ever stop crying. I held the pain in all its unbearable heaviness. Josh and Maggie held me in their arms and cried with me. They were powerless to change anything about our situation, but they willingly stepped into the darkness with me. I wasn't alone.

I was learning that pain demanded to be felt—on its own terms and in its own timing. It wouldn't be rushed. It wouldn't be pushed away or minimized. There was no set timetable for grief. There were no Bible verses or life truths that could lessen pain's grip. No matter how much I wanted to push it away or pretend it wasn't there, there were no tricks or tips to relieve the agony. Josh and Maggie knew I needed to allow my pain to wash over me like a tidal wave—that it would only begin to recede in its own time, bit by bit. At that moment, the only thing I could do was grieve, not knowing if hope would ever come.

Josh and Maggie honored my pain. They honored our tiny baby David and the difficult road ahead of him. They honored our broken hearts and lost dreams. They didn't minimize the journey before us with breezy advice or easy answers. They loved David exactly as he was—a whole soul inside a broken body.

Five days after David was born, Steve and I were still trying to absorb the shock of our new life. That morning, we ate some scrambled eggs and threw on our clothes. We made the short drive to the hospital and parked our car in what was becoming "our spot." I silently acknowledged the oak tree that watched us as we began another day at the hospital. We were beginning to establish a routine. I didn't want to live this new life, but what could I do? The old life and the old me were gone.

The hospital's automatic doors opened as we approached, and we were greeted by the familiar smell of antiseptic. We stepped into the elevator and pushed the button for the third floor. Before the doors closed, a nurse pushing a NICU crib joined us.

"Good morning," we said as we smiled. We had gotten to know the staff pretty well in a short time. As we chatted, I glanced down at the baby in the crib and realized it was David.

"Oh," I said, laughing, "that's David! That's our baby."

"I took him to radiology for an X-ray," the nurse explained. I suddenly felt a confusing mix of gratitude and anger.

How amazing it is to have good health care. I'm so grateful they are giving my baby what I can't give him. Our team of doctors and nurses are so thorough.

But then came the next thought.

How dare you? He is my baby—my baby! I want to know where he is at all times. I want to be asked before tests are run. I want to feel like a mother, not a casual bystander. I want to make decisions for my child. I want to be in control here.

But I *wasn't* in control. I *wasn't* a typical new mom. I was a new mom with a baby who had a lot of special needs. At every turn, I was confused and felt confronted by the heaviness and complexity of our situation.

Seven days after David's birth, we sat down with a geneticist to discuss his diagnosis. We had so many questions, and we faced a journey with so many unknowns. We peppered the geneticist with questions: "What did we do wrong? What will David's life look like? How severely is our son affected by this syndrome? Will David be okay? Are we going to be okay? What do we do next?"

The geneticist could have shared statistics or the latest research to answer our questions. Instead, he gave us deep insight into how to parent our new baby. Calmly meeting our eyes, he spoke tender words of profound truth. "You'll just have to get to know David to find out who he is."

It was impossible to say what David's life would look like. Even if we had a typical child, no one could tell us how intelligent, creative, determined, or successful he might be. The geneticist's advice was to love our son just the way he was, right at that moment.

After our conversation with the geneticist, Steve and I had some clarity. We asked each other if we were willing to love David as he was—with his disability, his small hand, his unknown future. In this moment, right now, do we love him? Yes, of course we do! It was simple and profound at the same time. Our conversation with the geneticist changed our perspective and gave us clarity. All we needed to do was get to know David right now, in that very moment. We didn't have to have everything figured out.

We weren't in control of the events leading up to David's birth. And we had no idea what the future held. But as we sat with the geneticist, we were given the best, most important advice any parent can receive—the most important advice any person can receive: *Love*. Love him just the way he is.

Something within me exhaled. We already had the one thing we needed most—love. I didn't know it yet, but our little David was going to teach us a new kind of love—a deeper and fuller love—and a brighter hope than we had ever experienced.

After two weeks in the NICU, we were itching to take our tiny baby home and begin real life as a family. Although not having the safety net of the hospital staff was frightening, we were tired of the beeps and buzzes and the smell of antiseptic. We were tired of the tubes and cords. We were ready to discover whatever our new normal might be.

The doctors explained that because David wasn't born with the reflex to suck, he would need a gastrostomy tube placed in his tummy before we could take him home. In a simple surgery, a small incision would be made in David's abdomen and a permanent tube would be inserted, enabling us to put food directly into David's stomach. The NICU doctor then explained that it would be three weeks before the surgeon could schedule the procedure. *Three weeks?* That felt like a lifetime! Despite various complications, including a heart defect and his very small size, David was medically stable. We wanted to take him home. Our parenting instincts kicked in. We were tired of waiting to be told what to do. We were tired of the hospital staff making decisions for us.

"Can I please have the surgeon's phone number?" Steve asked with determination.

With a little reluctance, the doctor scribbled down the surgeon's name and office phone number. Steve and I stepped outside the NICU doors, and Steve got out his cell phone. As he dialed the number, as he pushed each button on his phone, we were finding new strength.

"Good morning. Dr. Wright's office," the receptionist answered. "How may I help you?"

"Good morning," Steve replied, a tinge of anger in his voice. "My son is scheduled for G-tube placement surgery and we need to move up the date. We want to have the procedure done as soon as possible." He squared his shoulders, took a deep breath, and prepared for a fight.

"Oh sure, how about Tuesday?" the receptionist replied. That was only four days away! Steve's shoulders relaxed a bit, and I could feel our shared relief at her response.

"Yes, Tuesday would be wonderful," he told her.

"We'll see you then. Good-bye," she said and then hung up.

I looked at Steve with admiration. He was a new dad, but he knew how to fight for our baby. A wave of love swept over me. We had just won our first battle. We had taken charge, spoken up, and asked for what we needed. I knew there would be many more battles ahead of us, but in this moment, my heart rallied. We were stronger together encouraging each other to push forward, to advocate for David with all we had. As I witnessed Steve's strength, I felt a new strength of my own. We were David's parents, and we would not let him down.

The Unexpected Gift

"I have a gift for you," said the God of the universe. "I made this precious gift just for you. I'm giving you this gift because I love you."

I closed my eyes and held out my hands with anticipation.

What will it be? I wondered with childlike curiosity.

"Is it something wonderful, like traveling to a faraway country to see exotic and amazing things?" I asked God.

"No," he replied, "it's far more wonderful than that."

"Is it riches? I'll have a large home, fine clothing, lovely things?" I asked.

"No," he replied, "it's much finer than anything you can own."

"Is it beauty?" I asked. "Will I be graceful and pretty, with bright eyes and long legs?"

"No," he replied, "this gift is far more valuable than physical beauty."

"Is it wisdom?" I asked. "Will I understand the great schol- ars and philosophers?"

"No," he replied, "it isn't wisdom. Your gift will bring deeper insights than wisdom can provide."

"What is it?" I asked.

God placed the wrapped gift in my hands. This wasn't the gift I expected. I didn't understand it. It felt heavy—so heavy that I could hardly hold it.

"Don't unwrap it yet," God said. "When the time is right, you'll see the gift for what it truly is. Until then, trust me."

"This can't be my gift," I told God. "It's much too heavy for me to hold. It hurts when I hold this gift."

"You can't understand the gift yet," God explained. "But this gift is made just for you."

"I don't want this gift. Can I have a different gift? This gift is too much for me. This gift feels painful and raw. Please, God, anything but this," I pleaded.

God spoke soothing words to me in quiet, hushed tones. "Just wait," he said. "Just breathe. Just be. Trust me. I made this beautiful gift just for you. You think it's too heavy right now, but I will help you carry it."

"Okay," I finally agreed. "I will accept the gift. I don't want it. I don't understand it. But you are the God of the universe. You are a good and loving God."

I was surrounded by darkness. I felt afraid—nothing made sense. Those around me seemed to think everything was fine. Didn't they understand? Nothing was fine. I couldn't see the way forward.

"I know you can't make sense of this," God whispered. "I will help you carry this gift. I will direct you each step of the way. I will walk beside you, and soon you'll begin to see things clearly."

I held my gift and began to cry heavy, salty tears. The tears came freely, so freely that I wondered if they would ever stop. On and on they flowed—so many tears.

"Let the tears come," God whispered. "Every tear you cry makes room for more joy than you can imagine."

The ache in my heart was almost too much to bear. There were times I was sure my heart would break into a million tiny pieces. It was an ache so deep that it seemed to come from a place inside me I didn't know was there.

"I know you're hurting," God whispered. "This ache is because I am growing and stretching your heart to make room for a love deeper than you can imagine."

With time, my gift began to change me.

After a while, it didn't feel quite so heavy.

The tears made room for joy. So much joy.

My heart grew and stretched to make room for love. So much love.

As the darkness subsided, rays of light began to break through and something beautiful emerged.

Beneath the tears, heartache, and darkness, I saw my gift.

My gift was hope. So much hope.

It filled me up. My hope was light and bright and good.

"You had to walk through darkness to see the light," God explained. "You had to cry heavy, salty tears to make room for joy. You had to ache deep in your heart to know love. This was the only way you could know my true and lasting hope."

"Thank you," I said. "The darkness has subsided, and I can see more clearly. My tears have dried up and made room for joy. My heart is bigger, and I can love more deeply. I have hope, and hope is the most precious gift."

chapter eleven

COMING HOME

After three weeks in the hospital, we took David home at last. We felt like prisoners set free. We had shed the chains of hospital living and were taking control of our lives again—this time with our sweet baby in our arms. We buckled David into his car seat and slowly drove out of the hospital parking lot. I alternated between feeling shocked that they were letting us leave the hospital and hopeful that some sort of normal life might lie ahead.

We hardly knew our tiny baby. We had met him only a few weeks earlier and still felt inadequate for the task of caring for an infant with so many needs. Yet here we were, driving away from the hospital with our tiny David. We drove past that oak tree, leaving the hospital behind and stepping out into our new lives. The oak tree stood tall, watching us on our way out.

Shortly after we left the hospital campus, David made a gurgling/choking sound.

"Oh my gosh!" I yelled. "Pull over!"

Steve screeched over to the side of the road, and we both jumped out to see if David was still breathing. We opened the door to the back seat expecting to see the worst, but all we saw was our baby snuggled safely in his car seat looking content and calm.

We laughed nervously and tried to catch our breath. We slowly climbed back into our seats, realizing we were on edge. More than on edge, we were downright terrified. We were completely unprepared for the road ahead. Now that David was checked out of the hospital, no one would be there to remind us to feed him every three hours. No one would check to make sure we cleaned his G-tube area to prevent infection. No one would be there in the middle of the night if we needed help. We had fought to get David out of the hospital so we could bring him home, and now I wondered if we were up for the task.

We unloaded David and the diaper bag from the car and stepped into our apartment. I saw our apartment for the first time as part of a family of three. It was unnerving and exhilarating. The weight of our freedom and responsibility was both crushing and empowering. We were undone. We were scared out of our wits. But we were home. What was, was no longer. What would be, was filled with potential. Our new journey had begun.

The following days and weeks were a blur of sleep deprivation, medical appointments, and adjusting to being a family of three. David had terrible gas pain and reflux, common with his syndrome. There were days he seemed to cry nonstop. We fed him through the tube in his stomach and minutes later used the same tube to release gas that distended his abdomen and caused him to writhe in pain. We fed him every three hours, even through the night. Sometimes a feeding took a full hour—meaning that in two hours, we'd begin the entire process again. I was grieving, exhausted, and overwhelmed. I did not feel like myself.

We had been set free from the chains of the hospital. We were home and on our own—new parents finding our way. And yet I didn't feel free. I felt trapped inside my own fear—fear of the new world we found ourselves in, fear of my inability to keep my baby stable and healthy, fear of being left behind in a world that was moving on without us. We were home from the hospital, but not at home in our new lives. It would take time to find a new normal. It would take time to find myself again.

The Next Step

In the darkest times,
We see hope most clearly.
Hope illuminates the darkness.
Without hope we will stumble;
With hope we cannot see everything,
But we can see the next step.
All that is required
Is one thing—
The next step.

chapter twelve

TRYING TO FIND NORMAL

E verything was unfamiliar. Nothing was normal. I was disoriented and had no way to gauge my moods or energy level. I couldn't make sense of my feelings. What did it mean to be the mother of a baby with two fingers on his left hand and a feeding tube in his stomach? David was tiny, only about four pounds. He seemed so fragile. *What if I let him down? What if he dies?*

It seemed like the skies were gray every day, even if the sun was shining. My love for David often felt overshadowed by fear and exhaustion. I walked around in a fog and felt like I had heavy weights on my shoulders. There was a constant ache in my heart. I tried to do my best imitation of me, pretending to be a mom who was capable of caring for her newborn baby with a severe disability. I could sometimes manage a smile on the outside, but on the inside, I felt a crushing sadness.

One evening when David was just a few weeks old, I went from feeling stressed and sad to feeling completely overwhelmed. Steve was speaking at a church event, and I didn't want to call and interrupt him. When he'd left just an hour earlier, I'd assured him we would be fine. Then I fed David through his G-tube, and almost immediately he threw up the entire feeding. His most recent meal was all over my shirt, running down my neck and soaking into my bra. He was having horrible gas pain, and no matter what I did, his crying continued. I wanted to set him down for a couple minutes so I could at least change my top, but he continued to cry hysterically. On and on he cried until I felt like I was going insane.

I called my sisters, both of whom lived about twenty minutes away, to see if they could come over and help. Miraculously, they were both home and available. Within minutes, they jumped in a car together and headed my way. I couldn't believe how quickly they arrived. I handed one of them my tiny, hysterical baby and broke down into tears of frustration and exhaustion. *Will I ever be me again?*

I was a failure. I couldn't soothe my baby. What kind of a mother is incapable of comforting her baby? And this was my new life—not just a passing phase, but my new *forever. Will David cry every day for the rest of my life? Will he always struggle with this level of pain? Will I never be able to soothe my son?*

Then a terrible realization hit—David would never be able to tell me what was wrong. *Will every day be a guessing game of trying to meet David's needs?* As I sank lower into sadness, an even more painful thought crossed my mind. *Will my son never hug my neck or say the words, "I love you, Mommy"?* It felt like my heart was breaking physically as my body shook with sobs of desperation. It was a pain deep in my core. My soul hurt. I felt hopeless, heavy, and completely alone. And I felt like a fake, like the word *mother* would never apply to me.

Four close friends had given birth to healthy babies within months of David's birth, and I found myself feeling even more alone and on the outside. My baby was not like other babies.

He would not walk by his first birthday; the doctors told us he would never walk. He would not speak his first words at ten months; the doctors told us he would never speak at all. He was not able to breastfeed; he was fed through a tube in his stomach.

I was not like other mothers. I was not going to be babyproofing the house to keep an active toddler safe; I was not going to play groups; I was not rocking my baby to sleep for his afternoon nap. Instead, I spent my time wondering if David would ever eat by mouth instead of through a G-tube. I was driving him to medical specialists all over Southern California to see what surgeries would need to be scheduled for the next month. I was grieving, not celebrating. I wasn't adjusting to having a new baby; I was just trying to survive.

One night, we invited friends over for dinner, and I prepared one of our favorite dishes—cranberry chicken with rice. We made it through the salad, but just as we were about to serve the chicken, I looked at the clock and realized I needed to head to the back bedroom to pump breast milk for David's next feeding.

"Go ahead," I told them. "Don't worry about me. I'll be back in a bit."

From the bedroom, I could hear Steve and our friends laughing and talking as they enjoyed the meal. I felt completely and utterly alone—not only physically alone, but also emotionally isolated. This meal with friends represented my life—I got salad, but missed out on the main dish. I felt so hungry inside—hungry for normal, hungry for connection, hungry for my old life.

I sank back in the cozy chair in our bedroom and let a few tears slip down my cheek. Before David, I had only occasional and low-level stress—picking out what to wear or what to make for dinner was about as bad as it got. Now I was stressed constantly about life-or-death issues. I worried about whether my baby would stop breathing. I worried about whether my baby would ever eat by mouth. I worried about whether I would be swallowed up inside my sadness.

A couple days later, I was shopping for baby clothes when I ran into one of my former housemates. It had been a couple of years since we'd seen each other, and we hadn't kept in touch. She didn't know what was going on in my life, and I didn't know what was going on in hers. She looked the same, except she had an adorable, healthy baby cuddled next to her chest in a carrier.

My little David was tucked into his stroller and hooked up to his feeding tube. There was a bag of breast milk tied to the top of his stroller and a mess of tubing over his head. I'd concealed him by laying a blanket over the top of his stroller. The moment I saw her, I wanted to bolt in the opposite direction. I was not prepared to run into an old friend. How would I explain all that had happened since I saw her last? How could I describe the devastation that had engulfed our little family? I worried for me: *This is too much to handle.* I worried for her: *She can't handle this.* I worried for David: *He deserves to be celebrated, not hidden under a blanket.*

Before I could duck into the next aisle, she spotted me and came over, smiling. We chatted a few moments while I admired her baby. Then I took a step away, hoping this would be a brief encounter and we could say a quick good-bye. Perhaps I wouldn't have to explain David's special needs. Maybe I could avoid pulling back the blanket and exposing David to a world that might not accept him. Maybe I could escape without revealing my sadness and the rawness of my heart. But before I could make my getaway, she asked to see my baby.

I felt queasy. I wanted to explain that he had a disability, but I couldn't find the right words. I wanted to prepare her, but how? I wanted to run away, but I was trapped. As I pulled back the blanket, I saw a look of horror cross her face, which was then quickly replaced by a smile. I couldn't blame her. I looked down and saw David through a stranger's eyes—his body was surrounded by tubes; he had a hand with only two fingers; and at five pounds, he was still so tiny.

I smiled and did my best to give a quick explanation of David's special needs, but it felt so awkward. I did not fit. David did not fit. I could not make sense of things for myself, much less for anyone else. Once again, I felt ambushed by grief and by questions. *Who am I? Who is David? Who are we as a family? I don't know how to be me anymore. I don't know how to be the mother of a child with special needs. I don't know how to live my life.*

In that brief encounter with my old housemate, I spiraled down into a dark place—from surprise at seeing her, to a desire to avoid her, to shame over my baby with special needs and then to more shame for feeling shame, and finally to fear that this friend and others would never be able to walk this road with me. *Will I always feel so alone?* The hollow ache of loneliness overshadowed all the other feelings. It was a loneliness so intense that I wondered how much longer I could bear the weight of it.

My friend and I stood there chatting politely, trying to make the best of an awkward situation. After what felt like an eternity, we said good-bye, and I made my way through the checkout line and back to my car. I slowly buckled David into his car seat, climbed into the front seat, leaned my head on my arms over the steering wheel, and cried.

This is my new life, I thought as tears streamed down my face. *I will always be sad. I will always be overwhelmed. I will never fit in with other moms.*

The days drifted by and melded together. Even the days and nights blurred together, because Steve and I were up every couple of hours. We were so tired that we couldn't think straight. Exhaustion was our new normal.

One afternoon during this blurry time, our friends Karyn and Todd came over for a visit. Karyn had been my friend for a few years. We had taught together in the same school district and had both gotten pregnant at the same time. We were thrilled to be pregnant together, and our due dates were less than a month apart. But a few weeks into our journey, Karyn had a miscarriage. I cried with her and shared her pain. I also felt guilty that my pregnancy continued on. Now it was her turn to grieve with me.

Karyn and Todd were tender with David, gently holding him and stroking his head full of curly hair. If they were afraid, they didn't show it. If they didn't want to walk this journey with us, they were hiding it well. We talked and laughed. They were still themselves—the same friends we knew so well. We were still us, just a little bit broken as we began life with our new baby.

I caught myself in the moment; it felt almost . . . normal. I watched our friends love David and felt my own heart strengthen. For a moment, the loneliness subsided, and I felt a tiny glimmer of hope. *Maybe we aren't alone after all.*

Twice a week, nurses came to our home to weigh David and check his G-tube for any signs of irritation or infection. Other days, occupational therapists or physical therapists came to work with David. They gently moved his arms and legs—up and down, side to side, around and around—helping him stretch and increase his flexibility. They held him tenderly and talked to him. They smiled at him, looking at him without judgment. They weren't scared of his small hand with only two fingers. They weren't shocked by his G-tube. They weren't uncomfortable with his special needs. They were in their element—not only trained to do what they were doing, but also gifted with a passion for loving children with special needs.

We laid out a big blanket on the floor. Each therapist brought her own bag of toys. As they cooed and cuddled and played with David, I felt less alone. We were finding community. These therapists gave David not only love but also dignity; they affirmed that he was precious and valuable. Their presence in our home was water for my parched soul.

One therapist pulled out a rattle and began to shake it—first on the left side of David's head, and then slowly she moved the rattle to the right. "Did you see that?" she said with a big smile. "He moved his eyes toward the rattle! He was tracking the movement and the sound with his eyes." She was excited, and I felt it too—a small victory. It would be the first of many victories to come. I let myself feel a little joy.

While all of our home therapists had a calming and encouraging presence, there was one occupational therapist named Rochelle who bonded deeply with our family. When we met, I immediately felt drawn to her. She was smart and young, with an easy smile and soulful eyes. We talked easily, and I could be myself around her. After she had been working with David for a month or so, she told me that her son also had special needs.

"What?" I exclaimed. "He does? Tell me more! What kind of needs does he have?" All of a sudden, I had an ally. I no longer felt I was on an island alone. I wasn't the only mom who had a child with special needs. Help had come! I listened intently as Rochelle told me about her son.

"He has cerebral palsy," she explained. "He had a difficult birth and went without enough oxygen for a short period. He is five years old and relies on a wheelchair to get around. We still help him eat, but he's learning to feed himself. He can speak about twenty words but often communicates through pointing or a picture system. He's an amazing kid, and I just adore him. I'm honored to be his mom."

I'm honored to be his mom. Her words echoed in my head.

I tried to take it all in—not just what she had said, but also who she was. This capable young woman was not so different from me, yet she seemed full of life and joy and love. She was lighthearted and happy. She loved her son—so much that she said she would not change him. I wanted that too. Once again, I felt a tiny glimmer of hope.

On one of her visits, Rochelle told me a parable that moved my heart.

"When a child is born, God assigns an angel to watch over the new baby," she said. "This angel will stay beside the baby and comfort him. This angel will help the mother know when it's time to feed the baby, or change a diaper, or check on the baby in his crib. This angel is there to look after the baby, to nurture, to love, and to help keep him safe. God assigns each baby his or her very own guardian angel.

"When a special needs baby is born, all the guardian angels look on in awe, hoping God will choose them for this assignment. This baby is tiny; this baby may never walk; and this baby will have a harder life than most people. This baby will learn differently. This baby will need a lot of care. All the angels are eager to see who will be assigned to help watch over this precious new life. This baby will need an extra-special guardian angel.

"But time goes by, and God does not assign an angel to watch over this new baby with special needs. The angels look at each other, confused. *Surely God will assign one of us to watch over this baby,* they reason. *Surely God will not leave this baby without a guardian angel.*

"After a while, one of the angels works up the courage to ask God, 'Why haven't you assigned one of us to watch over this new baby? He has special needs. Surely this baby will need extra protection and extra nurturing.'

"The angels listen intently as God explains, 'None of you will be assigned to this baby. I have given this mother just what she needs to take care of her baby. This mother will be her baby's guardian angel.'"

Rochelle and I sat together quietly for a few moments. Her words stirred something deep inside me. While I didn't think that God was up in heaven literally assigning guardian angels to each baby (or maybe he was?), I felt the weight of my responsibility as David's mother, as well as an inner strength. I had been called to something extraordinary. It would take a lot of bravery and more strength than I thought I had, but God had entrusted me with this precious baby. He believed in me, and I was determined to do everything I could to love and nurture my child. I would keep him safe.

"You can do this," Rochelle told me as she gently touched my knee. "God has given you everything you need to be the perfect mother for David. You are his guardian angel. Just take it one day at a time, one moment at a time. You are an amazing mother, Lisa. You can do this."

I decided to believe her.

A few months after David's birth, I went back to work part-time. I was teaching special needs kids in our local school district. My younger sister Susan was a nurse. She stayed with David one day a week, feeding him though the tube in his stomach, changing his tiny diapers, and gently rocking him in her arms. Steve used his day off to care for David, burping him, holding him close in a front carrier while he did the dishes, and carefully using the

G-tube to keep David's tummy full. Our sweet baby was always in capable, loving hands.

My job gave me respite from the exhausting care David required. I got a little bit of breathing room, a little bit of normal inside our painfully unfamiliar world. Between work, therapy sessions, doctor visits, and trying to keep groceries in the refrigerator, I was going nonstop. Work felt easy compared to being a new mom. It was a chance to be me, just me—without all the heartache and confusion.

As we tried to find a new normal, we began taking little adventures as a family. One evening, we put David in a front carrier and went out to see a movie. He slept through the entire thing! We ate popcorn and gazed at the huge screen, and I could scarcely believe we were doing something so completely normal. What we once considered an ordinary Friday evening suddenly felt like an indescribable luxury. Steve and I felt like we had won the lottery.

"Can you believe it?" he said afterward. "We just went to the movies and ate popcorn!" Doing something normal felt exhilarating. We were lighthearted and hopeful. We were finding our way. We were making a life together as a family of three. We were falling in love with our little David.

When David was about three months old, I woke up one morning and felt different. I felt a lightness I hadn't felt in months, as if the clouds had parted and a bit of sunshine was peeking through at last. I felt like . . . me. Looking back on those days now, I realize that, in addition to all the grief, I had been suffering from postpartum depression. I wish I had known the signs and symptoms back then—maybe I could have gotten help to alleviate some of the pain. That morning, when a ray of light broke through the clouds, the depression began to subside. It felt like a rebirth of hope, raw and pure. I held on to it as tightly as I could.

Maybe, just maybe, I could still be me amid the craziness. Maybe, with all that I had lost, I did not have to lose myself. So far, our new journey had been full of pain, fatigue, and loneliness. But now I began to imagine that there might be more than just darkness ahead. We were still in one of the hardest times of our lives, processing the grief of raising a child with special needs and grappling with a host of unanswerable questions, but it seemed like maybe the dark clouds were at last beginning to part.

This Little Hand

This little hand was the first tangible sign that things were not as we expected.

This little hand, with only two little fingers, made my heart hurt and worry about the days ahead.

This little hand represented a syndrome and questions and the end of dreams I'd been dreaming for my tiny baby.

This little hand softly touches mine and reminds me that true beauty comes from within.

This little hand is teaching me that perfection isn't the goal; love is the goal.

This little hand is connected to this little body—a body that moves and explores and cuddles close to mine.

This little body has fought hard to overcome illness and disorder.

This little body holds the heart of my child. A heart that loves deeply. A heart that laughs with joy. A heart that doesn't worry about tomorrow, but finds beauty in this moment.

A heart so big and powerful that it has helped heal my own.

A heart that has taught me how to love better and more purely.

I wouldn't change this little hand, because it's part of the story that has brought us to today.

And today holds amazing, wonderful things.

The Love of a Mom

The love of a mom
Comes deep from inside.
It's a powerful force;
It's the wind on your side.

Her love is a gift
She gives every day
Through wisdom and insight,
Through laughter and play.

On difficult days
When the going gets tough,
Her words remind you,
"You are enough."

When all else fails,
When it all falls apart,
Her love is like glue
Healing cracks in your heart.

Through all kinds of weather,
No matter the storm,
Her love is a shelter,
A place to stay warm.

Mom's love is constant,
True and steadfast.
A love like no other,
It's a love built to last.

Thank you, moms,
For the love that you show.
It's the water and sunshine
That help us to grow.

chapter thirteen

A SPARK OF BRAVERY

One sunny Saturday when David was less than a year old, Steve and I decided to splurge and go to Baja Fresh for lunch. We couldn't really afford to eat out, but we needed to get out of the house. I gathered diapers and food for David in a bag while Steve strapped our still-tiny baby into his car seat, and we drove the short mile and a half to the strip mall for lunch. Steve parked and then pulled David's car seat out of the car, with David still buckled inside. He was cozy and happy in his little seat.

At the restaurant, we turned a high chair upside down to hold him and his car seat while we ate. If we were lucky, David would stay contentedly in his car seat while we ate. As I got David situated, Steve went up to order food—two steak burritos with rice and beans. I gave David a little kiss on the forehead and looked over toward Steve. Near him were two boys, about eight and ten, laughing and pointing at David. I couldn't hear what they were saying, but it seemed that they had noticed David's small hand with only two fingers, and they were nudging each other and gawking.

My cheeks flushed bright red and my heart shattered into

a thousand pieces. I wanted to climb under the table and hide. I wanted to grab David and run far away where no one would ever be mean to him. I wanted to protect him from a life in which the kids at school called him names and excluded him from their activities. Instead, I sat motionless as shame threatened to swallow me whole. But then a spark of bravery ignited somewhere inside me.

No, no, no! I am not ashamed of my son. Yes, he has only two fingers on his left hand. Yes, he is different. But he is amazing, and he is mine.

My first instinct was to grab those kids by their collars and scream, "How dare you laugh at my son! You are awful, terrible kids!" But in my heart, I knew. They didn't understand David. They had probably never seen a baby with seven fingers instead of ten. They were probably scared, so they were making fun of what they didn't understand.

Slowly, I unstrapped David from his car seat and carried him over to where the boys were now sitting with their parents. As I approached, I could see the look of terror on their faces. They probably thought they were about to be in big trouble. But instead, I calmly looked at the boys and said, "Hi, I'm Lisa, and this is my son, David. I saw that you noticed him, and I wondered if I could answer any questions for you." They looked back at me with blank expressions.

"Hello," the parents said warmly. "Thanks for coming over. He's adorable. How old is he?" They were incredibly kind.

We chatted for a minute or two while the boys stared blankly at David and me. Then I walked back to our table with my head held high and my chin quivering. It was terrifying, but I had been brave. I thought my heart would break when I saw those boys pointing and laughing at David, but I took a deep breath in and realized that my heart wasn't broken. I had been afraid that shame would swallow me up, but where was shame now? I didn't feel any shame at all. I felt pride.

I learned something about myself that I hadn't known when we left the house just a few minutes earlier. I wasn't powerless. I didn't have to sit by and let shame swallow me up. I didn't have to fear other people's opinions or judgment. I could stand up; I could be brave; I could speak my mind.

My chin was still quivering when Steve came back to the table with our burritos. With tears in my eyes, I told him what had happened. I looked at David, who was snuggled back into his car seat, and I felt overwhelmed with love for him. Maybe, just maybe, with a little bit of bravery, we could change the world, one conversation at a time.

I See a World

You are unique.
I am unique.
Each of us is unique in our own way.
There is no shortage of ways to be unique.
I see a world overflowing with unique individuals.

You deserve love.
I deserve love.
Each of us deserves love.
There is no shortage of love.
I see a world overflowing with love.

You feel compassion for my pain.
I feel compassion for your pain.

Each of us feels compassion for another's pain.
There is no shortage of compassion.
I see a world overflowing with compassion.

You have amazing ideas.
I have amazing ideas.
Each of us has amazing ideas.
There is no shortage of amazing ideas.
I see a world overflowing with amazing ideas.

You listen to my stories.
I listen to your stories.
Each of us listens to others' stories.
There is no shortage of stories.
I see a world overflowing with stories to be told.

You give kindness to me.
I give kindness to you.
Each of us gives kindness to each other.
There is no shortage of kindness.
I see a world overflowing with kindness.

You have a light to shine.
I have a light to shine.
Each of us has a light to shine.
There is no shortage of light in the world.
I see a world overflowing with light.

You comfort me when I cry.
I comfort you when you cry.
Each of us comforts others when they cry.

There is no shortage of arms to comfort each other.
I see a world of people who comfort each other.

You have hope.
I have hope.
Each of us has hope.
There is no shortage of hope in the world.
I see a world overflowing with hope.

You are enough.
I am enough.
Each of us is enough, just as we are.
There is no shortage of being enough.
I see a world overflowing with people who know they
        are enough.

chapter fourteen

A FAMILY OF FOUR

David was ten months old when I stared down at the positive pregnancy test. Steve and I felt like we had lived multiple lifetimes in those ten months. It was hard to even remember what life was like before David. We slept, showered, ate, gave David his medicine, fed him through his G-tube, and saw his therapists and doctors multiple times a week. We lived in the now, caring for our sweet David, finding our new normal. I was planning David's first birthday party, a chance to celebrate the amazing person he was, when we discovered we were pregnant.

We were simultaneously thrilled and terrified. Steve and I wanted another baby; we just hadn't expected it to happen so soon! As we began to tell our friends and family, we could see the look of shock on their faces. Weighing in at ten pounds, David was still so tiny. Most people thought it was too soon and probably too much for us to handle. We wondered the same thing, but here we were—pregnant with our second baby.

I made an appointment to see my doctor the following week. As Steve stood by my side, the doctor confirmed I was pregnant and told me this pregnancy would be considered high-risk. I actually felt grateful for the extra care that this designation entailed. I wanted to do everything we could to prepare for our second baby.

As we sat in the waiting room at the perinatologist's office, the door behind the receptionist's desk opened and a crying woman emerged. She tried to compose herself as she left the office, but it was obvious that she'd received bad news. One year earlier, I had been that woman.

I wanted to run to her. I wanted to hug her, comfort her, and tell her, "I know your world is falling apart, but you will find hope. I know it seems dark now, but you will find the light. I know you are grieving, but there is joy ahead."

I wished I could make it easier for her, but I knew I couldn't. Whatever news she had just received, she would have to walk her own path through the dark to find the light. She would have to grieve her own losses in order to heal. There was no way to expedite the pain. I reminded myself she would find her way, just like I was finding my way.

Nearly a year had gone by—a long year. It was a year full of grief, a year of finding a new kind of joy. It was a year spent learning how to navigate the medical system and how to care for our baby with special needs. It was a year spent falling in love with David.

I looked at Steve and thought, *The last time we were here, our world fell apart and our dreams shattered. But here we are again, pregnant with our second baby. We are different people than we were a year ago—a little more broken, a little softer, and a lot more aware that some things in our lives are utterly beyond our control.*

Please do not let this be twins, I prayed during one of our first ultrasounds. Since twins were so common in my family, it was a real possibility. I couldn't imagine caring for two tiny babies, plus our tiny David. When the doctor confirmed we were having only one baby, both Steve and I breathed a sigh of relief. One baby. We would soon be a family of four!

Two months later, when I was sixteen weeks along, Steve and I went to see the perinatologist—the same perinatologist we'd seen at the end of my pregnancy with David. The same one who'd said, "Expect problems." It had been almost exactly a year since we'd been in that office and had our lives turned upside down. No matter what news we got now, we wouldn't end the pregnancy, but we wanted to look closely at our baby's development. We wanted to know if our baby was healthy.

During the ultrasound, the technician counted every finger and every toe. She measured the baby's head and the bones in the baby's arms and legs. These details had somehow been missed in my first pregnancy. But now I wondered if maybe that oversight had actually been a gift. *Was it better not knowing something was wrong until just as David was being born? Was it easier to grieve with our sweet David in our arms instead of dreading the unknown for months?*

We knew from our previous experience that no matter how many tests and ultrasounds we passed with flying colors, the unexpected could still happen. But we hoped for good news. We hoped our second baby would be healthy. I had so many idealistic expectations when we prepared for David. With this pregnancy, I wanted to let go of expectations. I wanted this baby to be whomever he or she was, with no pressure to be someone we wanted or expected. No matter what, we would love this baby, just as we loved our precious David.

We got good news that day. Our baby looked healthy—ten fingers and ten toes. And we were having another boy. David would have a brother! We would call him Matthias, a Hebrew name meaning "gift from God."

Twelve days before Matthias was born, Steve started a new job in a town a couple of hours from where we were living. Since our move date was so close to my delivery date, we decided to use the same doctor who delivered David and scheduled an induction. Our new baby would be delivered a week early to make sure I didn't go into labor while we were in our new town, so far from our hospital. I liked having a plan. It gave me comfort. I would be induced at the same hospital where David had been born eighteen months earlier.

Even though I was thirty-seven weeks pregnant and we had just moved all of our furniture and stacks of boxes into our new home, I decided I wanted the house to be completely unpacked—no boxes, no newspaper—before we brought our new baby home. I wanted the boys' nursery to be adorable and ready for David and the new baby. I worked like crazy, unpacking box after box and trying to get every dish put away, every book on the shelf, every toy organized. Steve set up two matching cribs, and I made the beds with new baby sheets and handmade quilts from Chrissie. I hung some animal pictures on the wall and topped the dresser with a Humpty Dumpty lamp—the same lamp that had been in Steve's nursery when he was born. Our glider rocker was placed in the corner, the perfect spot to soothe and rock and read to both David and our new baby.

Three days before the induction, the house was completely unpacked and the nursery was ready. I was relieved, excited, and nervous.

Two days before the induction, I woke up around 3 a.m., climbed out of bed, and waddled into the living room. I made myself a bowl of chocolate ice cream with lots of chocolate syrup. I planned to watch HGTV into the early hours of the morning, enjoying a bit of alone time.

I was halfway through *House Hunters* and eating my middle-of-the-night dessert when I caught a slight movement out of the corner of my eye. I stood up and went to the dining room to look around. I didn't see anything, so I went back to the couch and resumed my TV watching. A few minutes later, something in the dining room caught my eye again. Now I was sure I had seen something. I stayed on the couch, silently watching and waiting. There it was again—something small and brown scurried quickly across the tiled floor. *Oh my gosh—it's a roach!* And not just any roach, a *giant* roach—bigger than a large paper clip.

I freaked out—sweating, heart racing, in full fight-or-flight mode. Then I tried to get hold of myself.

Lisa, you are growing a human inside you. You are caring for an eighteen-month-old with special needs. You have been brave through blood draws, invasive tests, and surgeries. You can deal with this roach. This is not a big deal.

I slipped off my flip-flop and inched closer to the most disgusting creature I had ever seen.

I can do this. I can do this. I can do this.

With all the courage and strength I could muster, I smacked down my flip-flop as hard as I could on top of the giant roach.

Smack! Its legs twitched and then went still.

I am a mama. Do not mess with me.

I left the roach on the field of battle, wiped off the bottom of my flip-flop, rinsed my hands, and went back to the couch. I figured I had done my part. Steve could sweep up the dead roach in the morning.

Wow, I am amazing! I thought, and I congratulated myself. *Seriously, is there anything I cannot do?*

The couple on *House Hunters* was touring house number three and weighing the pros and cons of each home they'd seen.

It was obvious that house number two was the best option—close to work with a great living room and backyard. "House two!" I called out loud to the couple on TV, just as I caught another blur of movement out of the corner of my eye.

No. Please, God, no.

Then I saw it—another large roach scurrying across the floor.

This. Is. My. Nightmare.

But I can do this.

"Be brave. Be brave. Be brave," I chanted aloud as I once more slipped off my flip-flop and inched closer to the ugly brown bug.

Smack! This one didn't even twitch. Instant death.

I stood quietly in the middle of the room. Waiting. Praying. Hoping it was the last one. But then I saw another. *Smack!* And another, and another. *Smack! Smack!* I waited, and the room was still. Then I waited longer, until I was sure that no more roaches were going to emerge.

At this point, I realized I couldn't leave our dining room littered with dead roaches. So I found our hand broom and dustpan under the kitchen sink and swept up the carcasses. There were eight in all.

I was praying this was the end of our roach problem when, you guessed it, out of the corner of my eye I saw another large roach scurry across the floor. First, a single tear rolled down my cheek, then another, and then I was sobbing. By the time I got to our bedroom to wake up Steve, I was hyperventilating.

"Babe," I choked out between sobs. "Babe, oh my gosh, babe, wake up."

I could not stop crying, and I could hardly catch my breath.

"What's wrong?" Steve jolted awake and jumped out of bed. He must have thought I was in labor or that David had stopped breathing or that there was an axe murderer in the house. I caught my breath long enough to say, "We have, we have, we have *roaches!*" Then I went back to sobbing.

"What?" he asked, trying to wake up enough to figure out what was really going on.

"Roaches!" I cried. "So many roaches! Every time I killed one, there were three more to take its place. *We have roaches!*" I screamed.

He tried to calm me down, and even though he hated roaches as much as I did, he came out to the dining room and began smashing the beasts with his flip-flop while I sat on the couch and continued to cry. After a good twenty minutes of flip-flop roach battle, he said, "Babe, we're not going to solve this problem tonight. Let's go back to bed. We'll have someone come in and take care of them for us."

We climbed back into bed, and I cried myself to sleep. I imagined a huge roach crawling near David's crib and felt nauseous. We could not bring our new baby home to a house filled with roaches.

The next day, Steve called an exterminator. They told us we would need to completely clear out all our kitchen cupboards top to bottom, bag up all our food, and seal all toys, towels, and bedding into huge plastic bags. In other words, we needed to pack up the house—the house we had just unpacked. Then we needed to be out of the house for six hours while they sprayed and let the poison settle into the cracks and crevices of each corner and floorboard.

We were having a baby in two days, and just the day before, I had finished washing and organizing our entire kitchen, organizing the boys' toys, and putting clean sheets in the boys' cribs. But we had no choice. We pulled all the flattened boxes out of the garage, taped them together again, and began wrapping and packing every single dish and pan we had just unpacked. My sisters came over to help us undo what we had just done. Steve scheduled the exterminators to come while I was in the hospital delivering Matthias.

Two days later, I was admitted to the hospital and taken to a private room. I changed out of my regular clothes and into my hospital gown.

Here we go. Please, God, let this baby be healthy.

The nurse came in and ran the first stress test to check the baby's heart rate. Everything was as it should be. The doctor administered Pitocin to get my labor started, and soon afterward, I was given an epidural to help with the pain. Labor came easily and progressed quickly. After the epidural, my pain was minimal and I enjoyed talking with Steve and my sisters as we waited for labor to progress. Soon it was time to push, and with just a few pushes, we welcomed our beautiful, blue-eyed baby into the world. He was pink and healthy. A wave of relief washed over me.

He is perfect. Thank you, God. Thank you!

Then came another wave of emotion, fast and unexpected, knocking the breath out of me. Guilt.

Do I love this baby more because he doesn't have a disability? Am I betraying David by loving our new baby?

As I held Matthias in my arms, I looked down at his perfectly round head and rosy cheeks. He was healthy and strong and normal. David was tiny and weak with a disability. Matthias had a robust cry that could be heard even into the hallway outside our hospital room. David had made no sound when he was born, not even a whimper. Matthias was a healthy seven pounds, eight ounces. David had been a frail four pounds, two ounces. Matthias was the baby I expected when David was born. His was the birth I had prepared for. He was the baby we had wanted.

I looked down at the beautiful boy swaddled in my arms. He was only minutes old.

You are everything I wanted. You are everything I hoped for. This is my redo. This is the delivery I was supposed to have eighteen months ago. But instead of feeling blessed, I felt like I was betraying David.

Matthias latched on immediately and started breastfeeding. David had never latched on. I'd been afraid I might hurt him, but now I regretted that I never once tried breastfeeding him. I wished I had at least tried. I wished David and I could have bonded this way in his first days.

I felt overwhelmed by shame.

How can I love and care for two babies who are so different? How can I love Matthias and meet his needs without betraying David? How can I love David and meet his needs without neglecting Matthias?

I was tired, so very tired. It felt so good to lie in my hospital bed and sleep. I did not have to unpack boxes. My sister was caring for David, and the nurses helped Steve and me with Matthias. I closed my eyes and tried not to think about the unknown. I tried not to think about what needed to be done. I tried not to think about anything.

I wanted to be alone. I wanted to lie in this bed for the rest of my life.

Can I just stay here forever?

A couple days later, we made the two-hour drive back to our new home with our two babies. David was eighteen months old, and for a short time, he looked like a giant next to our newborn. Matthias was sleeping in his car seat as we pulled into the driveway of our home.

Steve parked and suggested that I stay with the babies while he went inside to clean up after the exterminators. I imagined the roach carcasses littering our home and happily waited in the car. Turning around to look in the back seat, I tried to take in the beauty and goodness of these two incredible humans entrusted to my care.

Am I up for the task? I wondered, with serious doubts.

Steve went from room to room with the hand broom and dustpan, searching under the table and chairs, in corners, and under the couch, sweeping up every single roach. As far as I was concerned, he may as well have been wearing shiny armor and riding a white horse—he was my hero. When he was done with the cleanup, he came outside to help with the boys and the bags.

"It will be okay," he gently reassured me as we unbuckled the boys from their car seats and carried them into the house. I didn't know if he was talking about our recent roach problem or transitioning to having two babies. Either way, I hoped he was right. I wanted us to thrive as a family of four. Everything was still so unfamiliar and unknown. I had nothing figured out. I felt like an imposter in my own life. Still, his words reassured me, and I hoped it truly would be okay.

I can do this. I can do this. I can do this.

We had been in our new house for just two weeks. We had a kitchen to unpack (again) and floors and surfaces to wipe clean from fumigation residue. We had two babies, one with special needs and the other a stranger to me, a beautiful boy I'd met just two days earlier. Steve held the front door open as I took a deep breath and entered our new home with our new babies, eager to begin our new journey as a family of four.

Guilt and Grace

Guilt criticizes;
Grace affirms.

Guilt says do more, be more;
Grace says be still and rest.

Guilt is a liar;
Grace is a truth-teller.

Guilt condemns;
Grace forgives.

Guilt screams and yells;
Grace whispers kind words.

Guilt gives up;
Grace moves forward.

Guilt brings despair;
Grace brings hope.

Guilt scratches and claws;
Grace soothes and comforts.

Guilt piles on;
Grace lightens the load.

Guilt points the finger;
Grace is a hand to hold.

Guilt rolls its eyes;
Grace smiles with warmth.

Guilt says you'll never be enough;
Grace says you are enough, just as you are.

chapter fifteen

THINKING OUTSIDE THE BOX

If David was teaching us to let go of expectations, Matthias was teaching us to ignore them altogether. You've heard of people who march to the beat of their own drum? Matthias threw the drum out the window and picked his own instrument. And not just any instrument, but something like an Australian didgeridoo. From the very beginning, this was a kid who knew how to be uniquely himself—someone who naturally thinks outside the box and walks his own road. Someone who loves and embraces the person he was made to be.

When we brought Matthias home from the hospital, we were initially caught off guard by how different his needs were from David's. David had been so tiny when we brought him home from the hospital that his cry was barely a whisper. Matthias came home *loud*. We joked about being wakened in the night, not by a fussy baby, but by a newborn who could go from complete silence to bloodcurdling scream in a split second. Once again, this was a whole new world, and we were trying to make sense of unfamiliar surroundings. We loved and adored Matthias; we simply had no idea how to take care of a typical newborn.

Introducing another baby into our family—a baby with needs so different from David's—was more chaotic and draining than I expected. I was learning how to breastfeed for the first time, and learning how to read Matthias's cues. *Is he hungry? Is he tired? Is he wet, poopy, in pain?* He was a stranger to me. Those first weeks were especially exhausting and intense. Steve had just started a new job. We had just bought our house, moved, and unpacked (twice). We were also still sweeping up dead cockroaches. We didn't have friends or family nearby. I felt overwhelmed and lonely, tired and confused. But slowly, we started to find our way as a family of four.

When Matthias was about a week old, he screamed at the top of his lungs in the middle of the night. I was so exhausted that I lifted him out of his crib and cuddled him in bed with us while he latched on and fell asleep. That night was the beginning of Matthias sleeping in our room for years. He would fall asleep in his own bed and then at some point in the middle of the night find his way into bed with us. It may not have been ideal, but we were in survival mode. We did what we had to do. And I learned to never underestimate the power of cuddles—cuddles are a good thing.

When Matthias was three years old, we got him a Big Wheel tricycle. Remember those? The ones with a huge front wheel and small back wheels, made of blue, red, and yellow plastic? My siblings and I had raced Big Wheels around our cul-de-sac, pedaling fast and then slamming on the brakes to skid out. We had so much fun. I imagined Matthias would have a blast riding his Big Wheel up and down our long driveway—maybe even down our dirt road when he got a little bigger.

Of course, Matthias had different ideas. I don't think he ever once *rode* that Big Wheel. Instead, he carried it around the backyard, turned it upside down, put his hands on each of the pedals, and spun them round and round. He pulled out his tiny Hot Wheels cars and sent them careening down the plastic slope of the bike frame so they'd crash into the concrete patio. He played with that Big Wheel for hours, but never in the way it was intended to be played with. Matthias always thought outside the box. He did things his own way—and we loved that about him.

Matthias was still three when he started drawing. He packed his own bag with pencils and paper and carried it with him everywhere we went—something he continues to do to this day! At fourteen, he's been drawing now for ten years, hours every day—and he's good at it. I have a video of Matthias at seven telling me he was "born to be an artist." Maybe he was. I wait with anticipation to see who he will become.

When he was five years old, we were invited to an "art party" for a set of twins in his kindergarten class. We gathered at a local art studio, where the kids were going to have snacks and cupcakes, and a teacher would lead them through a painting project.

Matthias walked into the studio, looked around the room, and then went straight to the host, the mother of the twin girls. "Where is your husband?" he asked.

"Oh, he's home sick today," she explained with a smile.

Satisfied with her answer, Matthias headed over to the snack table for some goldfish crackers. The host and I both laughed. What five-year-old notices something like that? And what five-year-old refers to a friend's dad as "your husband"? Matthias has always been an old soul, wise and insightful beyond his years.

Around this same time, we took a field trip to a local pumpkin patch with Matthias's class. Thirty students hopped into the school bus, giddy with excitement. At the pumpkin patch, there were bright orange pumpkins of all shapes and sizes. After wandering through the corn maze and a very tame haunted house, each child got to pick out his or her very own pumpkin. Then the class filed back onto the bus and returned to the school. After settling back into the classroom, the teacher asked, "What was your favorite part of our field trip today?" All hands shot into the air. The teacher called on Matthias.

"I enjoyed watching our class get off the bus at the school," Matthias said, in a very grown-up, matter-of-fact tone. "When we lined up with our pumpkins and walked back to the classroom, it was like a pumpkin parade!"

The teacher smiled and nodded and made eye contact with me. Later, she told me she had never had a student who saw the world the way Matthias did. He was one of a kind.

Matthias has a vivid imagination. For years, he dressed as a superhero every day. He wore a blue superhero cape with a large *M* on it, mismatched rubber boots (one frog boot, one yellow boot), a Batman mask, and an oven mitt on each hand. Attired in superhero glory, he felt confident and powerful. He knew he looked *awesome.* He would walk proudly into the grocery store or Barnes & Noble, completely unaware of the adults smiling fondly in his direction. Perhaps he was used to people looking at us because his older brother had two fingers. Whatever the reason, he was wholly unself-conscious. I loved every minute of it.

As I was learning to let David be David—to love him just as he was—I was also learning to let Matthias be Matthias, to celebrate him for who he was. I have two incredibly unique boys, each with their own needs and quirks, their own personalities. From the day they were born, they have been teaching me not only what it means to be true to who I am, but that I am lovable just as I am. My *best* me is just who I was made to be.

They have taught me what it means to love and be loved— without expectation, without needing to change, without earning.

They continue to teach me what it means to love and accept myself just as I am—without judgment or criticism. I still have so much to learn, but I *am* growing. Perhaps someday I'll be brave enough to wear whatever my Batman mask oven mitt equivalent is and walk around with my head held high, confident that my truest self looks awesome. Until then, I watch both my sons with awe and admiration.

Artist (A Poem for Matthias)

With pencil in hand,
Sketching and knowing.
You have a gift,
Stretching and growing.

Keep on practicing.
Refining with time.
Seeking inspiration,
What will you find?

Looking from all sides,
Seeing with new eyes.
Bravely creating,
Ignoring the lies.

Taking a risk,
Moving boldly forward.
Fear takes a back seat,
Your goal moving toward.

The ideas in your mind
Combine with your heart.
Sharing with the world
Your own kind of art.

Inventing something new,
Be it grand, be it small.
What begins with you
Will belong to all.

Giving the world
What only you can,
You are an artist
With pencil in hand.

chapter sixteen

BECOMING MY TRUEST SELF

I adored our family of four. We had two happy, silly, lovable boys who were just beginning preschool and kindergarten. Steve and I were starting to feel like real adults, with jobs and kids and a house to take care of. Life was complicated, but beautiful. We each had our own personalities and quirks, which was wonderful, but also complicated. We each had our own needs and wants. David had a disability, which meant he needed to be fed, diapered, and assisted with most activities. Matthias and David had overlapping needs when they were babies and toddlers, but increasingly different needs as they grew. I cherished their uniqueness, but often felt torn trying to meet their differing needs.

It seemed like there was always someone who needed my attention. I wanted to give each of my boys—my sons and my husband—what they needed, but that required more time and energy than I had. So I defaulted to my old strategy of setting myself aside. I had been setting my own needs and wants up on a high shelf since I was a girl, and I was good at it. It all started when I stopped fighting for the red bowl. That's when I first trained myself to stop needing and wanting things. That's when I bought into the lie that if I could make other people happy, they would love me.

In our little family of four, denying my needs and wants meant there was one less complicating factor to manage, one less person to worry about. Plus, I reminded myself that I was doing a good thing by loving and serving others. I felt confident that this would not only make my boys happy but also fill my heart and make me happy. Best of all, if everyone was happy, I would be okay. I would be enough. I would be lovable. Deep down, that's what I really wanted—to be loved.

I made it my twofold mission to love and serve my family and to ignore my own needs and wants. We were creating a meaningful life together. We were making a beautiful home. We ate chocolate chip pancakes on Saturday mornings and read books together at bedtime. We were building a jewelry business that was growing year by year. What had started as a creative hobby at our kitchen table was requiring more of our time and attention—more about this later. Occasionally, Steve and I went out for a date night or enjoyed a rare weekend away. Sometimes I even treated myself to a pedicure.

Although we had finally found our way into a new normal, I felt tired and, to be honest, increasingly bitter. I resented that the boys and Steve took and took from me, never considering my needs and wants. There were times I thought they didn't recognize or appreciate how much I sacrificed for them. In my frustrated moments, I felt like they were ungrateful. These feelings ebbed and flowed. There were also occasional moments when the house was clean and the fridge was full, when the boys were happy and Steve and I felt connected. In those moments, I could exhale. Everything was all right. I was doing a good job. I was a good wife and mom. I was lovable. But those moments were fleeting. Soon the house would be messy again; the fridge would need to be restocked; someone would get upset; Steve and I would disagree. Then I went back to feeling like a failure. Nothing was right. I wasn't doing a good job. I was a bad wife and mom. I wasn't lovable.

I felt like I had spent my entire life chasing after those brief moments when I could exhale, and now I was tired of chasing. I was tired of feeling like there wasn't enough space for me. I was tired of feeling like a failure. I was tired of going and going and going. I wanted space. I wanted to rest. I wanted it to be okay to be me; I just didn't know how.

I remember a lesson David taught me on a sunny Sunday morning a couple of years ago. We arrived at church a few minutes early. David held my hand as he slowly climbed the front steps of the church, one at a time. Once inside, he pulled away from me. He wanted to explore the sanctuary before the service began.

David was nonverbal, but we were learning that he still had much to say. He communicated by taking our hands and leading us to what he wanted. He spoke through gestures, physical touch, and heart connection. I followed him around the sanctuary as he slid his hand over the smooth wood of the church pews, weaving in and out of the narrow spaces. Then he crossed the aisle and made his way over to a woman sitting by herself. She looked to be in her late thirties, and she had a kind face and a gentle presence.

We had never met this woman, but that didn't stop David from approaching her. He was rarely shy and seemed to have a knack for approaching people who were warm and loving. As he got closer, the woman looked up and smiled at him. Once beside her, David turned around and backed up to her—his way of asking to be held.

"He wants to sit on your lap," I explained. "He can sit next to you if you prefer."

"No," she said, "I'd love to hold him." She carefully lifted him onto her lap. He tenderly wrapped his arms around her neck and laid his head against her shoulder.

"Is this okay?" I asked, anxious to be considerate of her. "Would you like me to move him?" She looked up at me with tears in her eyes.

"My mom was diagnosed with cancer a couple days ago," she said in a quiet voice. "I just needed a hug so badly. He knew exactly what I needed."

I knelt beside them and touched her knee softly as she and David embraced. It was a holy moment of connection that soothed her hurting heart. In that moment, David, who had a disability and was nonverbal, poured out love to a stranger, offering her comfort and connection.

I immediately thought about the soul connection I'd had with Trent, the student who had read my mind. I thought about the deep connection I had with Chrissie. I thought about how much I loved David and how our hearts knew each other well. Kneeling beside them, I watched David and his new friend embrace, and I witnessed their souls connecting.

David, my gentle teacher, was showing me how to be my truest self. I simply needed to listen to my heart and consent to be me. In this holy moment, something clicked.

I did not have to be good enough.

I did not have to be kind enough.

I did not have to be perfect.

I did not have to try so hard.

I had nothing to prove. I simply needed to be *me*. I was already lovable. From this place—just being me, my true self—God does the work of meeting needs. God used David to pour out love on this hurting woman. God had given David a beautiful heart.

David didn't question his worth or value; he simply allowed God to work through him as he was. God had also given me a beautiful heart, the truest part of me. Instead of ignoring my heart, I wanted to listen to it. I wanted to care for my heart and nurture it.

In that moment, I was beginning to see that I needed a whole heart so it could overflow with love for others. And I was beginning to wonder if all I needed to do was follow David's example—to show up and allow the God of the universe to do amazing things through me. *Could it be true? If David was just being himself, could I just be me—the me God made me to be, my truest self?* I wanted to believe it; I was beginning to believe it.

That day, I took my first steps on a new path—a path toward being my truest self. I did not know it yet, but this path would get much rockier before it got smooth again. It would not be easy to become a whole person who could acknowledge her needs and wants. It would not be easy to let go of my desire to please others and make them happy. I would walk through dark times before I could see the light. But God had given me a glimpse of freedom, a peek into what it looked like to just be me.

I wanted more space in my life, more beauty in my life, more *me* in my life. I wanted to become my truest self.

Your Smile (A Poem for David)

Like golden rays when the sky breaks apart
Or glue healing the cracks in my heart.

Like a long walk together holding hands
And barefoot steps along the softest sands.

Like the scent of summer filling the air,
The saltwater wind blowing through my hair.

Like hopeful news after weeks of waiting
And a melody that's captivating.

Like waking up after a good night's sleep
Or a silent promise we two will keep.

Like all in this world that is good and true,
Unwrapping a present shiny and new.

Like finding hope where least expected,
Being safely from the storm protected.

Like exhaling and breathing new air,
Gazing at something amazing and rare.

Like what was broken has been made whole,
It's a peek into your beautiful soul.

Like a sigh of relief, peace in knowing
We'll be together, wherever we're going.

Like two hearts each other befriending
And a story with a happy ending.

Your smile is magic, simple and pure.
I've seen it firsthand, so I know for sure.

chapter seventeen

BEAUTY MATTERS

When I was nine years old, my mom took me shopping for new shoes one afternoon. My old shoes were worn out and too small, and it was time for a new pair. As we entered our local Payless shoe store, I spotted a pair of emerald green flats and fell in love. Those shoes were going to change my life.

"Please, Mom," I begged.

"They're not very practical," she answered. "Do you promise you'll wear them?"

"I promise," I said.

We drove home, and I skipped into the house, thrilled with my new green shoes. I could hardly believe I owned something so beautiful. They were mine, all mine! I loved the feeling of owning something so beautiful.

I wore them, even though they gave me blisters. I wore them when the color scuffed off around the toes. I wanted to hold on to them tightly, to keep them forever, but their beauty faded, and they eventually wore out.

I felt a little sad a year later when we cleaned out my closet and bagged up those green shoes, along with other too-small or no-longer-needed items. But it wasn't long until something else caught my beauty-hungry eye.

A couple weeks later, my friend Marie invited me to her house to play. When she opened her bedroom door, my eyes beheld the most glorious sight—a four-poster bed with a white ruffle canopy. It was so beautiful I could hardly stand it.

It was the first time I remember feeling envy. I wanted that bed to be mine, but I knew that no matter how much I begged and pleaded, my parents would never buy me a four-poster bed with a ruffle canopy.

My encounter with Marie's four-poster bed with a ruffle canopy would not be the last time I would feel jealousy and longing. I tried to fill my heart with pretty things, but just like my emerald flats, their beauty faded. Nothing seemed to keep that jealous ache away for long.

As I became an adult, I continued to crave beauty.

I dreamed of creating a beautiful life complete with a lovely home, a fine-looking husband, and adorable children. Maybe a white picket fence to finish it off. The day David was born, my dreams crumbled. We had a baby with two fingers. David wore his brokenness on the outside. But I still wondered, *If I try really, really hard, can I still make our lives beautiful? If I can create beauty out of the mess, maybe I can make everything okay. Maybe I can make a different kind of beautiful.*

In this new fantasy of a beautiful life, I would be an amazing mom who effortlessly raised two sons, one of whom had special needs. Everyone would marvel at how easy I made it look. We would have delicious homemade dinners in our cozy home. Steve and I would have a marriage that grew stronger every year. I wanted to create this beautiful life, and I was trying to live out this new fantasy, but it wasn't working. It may have looked beautiful on the outside, but on the inside, it was empty.

As I fell in love with David, I felt guilty for still wanting more. Shouldn't I just focus on being grateful for was given to me, for what I already had? I began to believe that my pursuit of beauty was self-indulgent. Even though I craved it and spent hours creating it, I felt guilty for "wasting" my time on something so frivolous.

Maybe beauty is a luxury. Maybe I don't even deserve it.

The tighter I tried to hold on to beauty, the more it seemed to slip through my fingers.

The more I looked to beauty for fulfillment, the emptier I felt.

The more I tried to portray a certain image, the more frustrated I became.

When I looked for fulfillment in outward expressions of beauty—my home, my children, and material things—I felt only inner conflict. Material things were never going to bring me peace or satisfy my soul. I knew that, but I kept reaching for beautiful things. I was trying to control things beyond my control. I was trying to use outside things to change inside things.

Beauty was around me. I could see it, appreciate it, enjoy it, but when I tried to hold on to it, it vanished. I wanted the perfect life, even though I knew life was imperfect. I wanted beauty to make me whole, make me valuable, make me better—but that isn't what beauty is for.

What is beauty? I began to look for it. I tried to see with new eyes and open hands. I did not try to control it or own it; I simply tried to notice it.

When David was three months old, he laughed for the first time. It was a rolling giggle, and it was the most incredible sound we had ever heard. Steve and I looked at each other with unbridled joy. It was beautiful.

When David was eighteen months old, his brother, Matthias, was born. We were relieved to meet our healthy, happy baby. Matthias balanced out our family. God knew that Matthias was exactly what we needed. He was beautiful.

Life was messy and imperfect. We were exhausted, and learning how to care for two babies required a steep learning curve. But there we were, an imperfect but beautiful family of four. We had two amazing boys to call our own.

We bought our first house and filled it with thrifted furniture we sanded and painted ourselves. We bought towels to coordinate with the ugly peach tile in the bathroom—and somehow it worked. Every Saturday morning, we brought the boys into our bed and snuggled. When they got restless, we went to the kitchen and made pancakes drenched with syrup and dusted with powdered sugar. These moments weren't fancy, but they were beautiful.

Money was especially tight when the boys were young. We managed to pay our bills every month, but we had little left over for fun. Sometimes we splurged and went to Dairy Queen for chili cheese dogs. I treasured those memories with the four of us sitting in the booth at DQ. These were simple, beautiful moments.

During a particularly difficult financial time, someone from our church slipped $500 into Steve's briefcase. We were in shock. To this day, we have no idea who gave us that money. It was one of the most humbling gifts we ever received. It was truly beautiful.

Sometimes I drove to the ocean's edge with the boys. We parked and rolled down the windows, letting the sea breeze blow through our car as we stared out at the glittering ocean waves. I inhaled deeply, filling my lungs with the salty ocean air. My heart was happy. It was beautiful.

When David was seven and Matthias was five, Steve and I were in their shared room one night getting them ready for bed.

The boys each had their own toddler bed on opposite sides of the room. We each took a child, pulling off playclothes and putting on pajamas. As I finished up and helped Matthias choose a couple of books for a bedtime story, David did something incredible and brave. From his toddler bed, he took a few steps across the room without holding on to anything. Steve and I completely freaked out.

We had been working for years to build up David's leg muscles and help him balance. He had learned to use a walker—we called it his red racer—around the house and at school. With his red racer, he could turn corners and move independently. Every day, the school staff worked with him to increase his confidence.

When David was born, we had been told he would likely never walk, but we held out hope. We prayed he would not only learn to walk, but also someday learn to run. In the meantime, we held on to his arms and celebrated every step he took with assistance. Day by day, he grew stronger and more stable. When he learned to use his red racer independently, we were elated. On this very special evening, we clapped and cheered when he took his first steps without help. David was all smiles. He was walking—all by himself!

We placed him next to his toddler bed again, and off he went, taking five or six steps to cross the room to Matthias's bed. Over and over, he put one foot in front of the other, confidently taking steps without help. It was incredible. It was monumental. It was one of the most beautiful things I had ever seen!

I had experienced true beauty, yet so much of my time and energy was being spent trying to manufacture a certain kind of beauty—a beauty that was surface-level, a beauty I could control, a beauty that would make others love me. As I pursued this surface beauty, I felt a nagging sense that something was wrong, something was "off."

I should be cleaning closets, not going in search of another treasure, I scolded myself as I scoured our local thrift store.

When I sanded a used dresser and painted it red for the boys' room, I had a nagging sense that my priorities were all wrong.

Setting the table with our good dishes, pretty napkins, and candles was just silly if it was only the four of us at home.

My heart craved beauty, hoping it could fill me. But deep down, I knew that wasn't beauty's job.

God was working in my heart, and I began to rethink my perspective on beauty. I realized that I had been using beauty as a measure of my worth, a tool to feel "good enough." I wanted beauty, not so much because it gave me joy, but because I thought it would make me better, make me more valuable. If I could be beautiful enough, maybe I would be more lovable. But a perfectly designed home, perfectly behaved children, and a properly set table never made me feel more valuable or lovable. In fact, those pursuits were actually creating walls between me and those I loved.

I was finally beginning to understand that outward beauty wouldn't fill me, wouldn't make me good enough. I could see that these precious moments and beautiful memories were worth far more than what other people thought about me.

I was learning that beauty couldn't be owned or possessed.

Beauty came to me when I opened my eyes and opened my heart.

Beauty came to me when I stopped trying to control things and let them be what they were—messy and amazing.

There was nothing wrong with emerald green shoes or four-poster beds with ruffle canopies. There was nothing wrong with painting a used dresser to give it new life or setting the table with good dishes and pretty napkins. These are beautiful gifts—ours to enjoy for a while. But a smile, a tiny giggle, an anonymous gift, my child in my arms, his first steps, the ocean waves, coffee with a dear friend—these are the most beautiful gifts of all.

I wanted to hold beauty with open hands. I wanted to remind myself that, although I could not own it, there was no shortage of beauty in the world. It was impossible to run out of beauty because the God of the universe had filled his creation with beautiful things.

My perspective on beauty was changing, but my heart still lagged behind. I wasn't sure how to let go of trying to be enough. *What if I let go and find out I'm not lovable? What if I stop trying to control everything and then our whole world falls apart?* I was surrounded by beauty, but I continued to fear it wasn't enough.

Deep down, I was afraid *I* wasn't enough.

I Held My Heart

I took care of my body.
I ate healthy foods; I walked every day.
I found the right lipstick; I bought the perfect jeans.
This is good, I thought. But it wasn't enough.
I held my heart, and it was empty.

I got married; we had two amazing children.
I was a loving mother, firm and fun.
We made pancakes every morning and read stories before bed.
This is good, I thought. But it wasn't enough.
I held my heart, and it was empty.

I made a cozy, beautiful home.
I saved for a couch and throw pillows. I kept it tidy.

I invited friends over for dinner, and we talked late into the night.

This is good, I thought. But it wasn't enough.

I held my heart, and it was empty.

I started a handmade business.

I created jewelry; people wore it.

I wrote words; people read them.

This is good, I thought. But it wasn't enough.

I held my heart, and it was empty.

I went to church every Sunday.

I read my Bible and prayed consistently.

I tried to love others; I tried to be spiritual.

This is good, I thought. But it wasn't enough.

I held my heart, and it was empty.

I broke down.

I sat alone in a quiet corner while tears fell.

In my desperation, I called out to the God of the universe.

"I've done all these things, but my heart is empty. I need you."

"You are good," he said. "You are enough."

Then he whispered, "All you need I have given to you. Come to me empty-handed and open-hearted."

He held my heart, and it was full.

chapter eighteen

STRETCH AND TRY

In 2001, shortly before I got pregnant with David, Steve and I took a weekend trip to San Diego with friends. We explored, ate good food, and spent a lot of time talking and laughing. One afternoon, we strolled around Coronado Island and walked through a few charming boutiques. In one of the shops, I found some handmade bracelets—freshwater pearls and sterling silver beads strung on stretchy elastic and priced at $22 each or two for $40. With our tight budget, they were pricey, but I decided they would make a lovely souvenir of our weekend. I purchased two and slid those dainty bracelets right onto my wrist.

Later that evening, I remembered visiting bead stores in high school. They smelled like patchouli and were filled wall to wall with beads—from tiny to extra-large. My friends and I spent hours together selecting beads, paid around twenty-five cents apiece for them, and then went home to string them into a necklace or bracelet.

I bet I could make these boutique bracelets for a lot less than I paid for them.

The Monday morning after our weekend getaway, I slipped the bracelets onto my wrist as I was getting ready for work.

I decided I would head to a craft store later that day in search of materials to re-create these beautiful bracelets. I felt inspired. Our apartment was full of creative projects—a footstool I'd re-covered, a dresser I'd painted, and a journal I'd decoupaged—so finding another creative project was right in line with how I liked to spend my free time. I was just like my mom and my grand-mother, who had always been looking for a new creative project.

I played with the bracelets all day, stretching the elastic and running my fingers over the smooth freshwater pearls. I had dreamed about starting my own business someday. *Could I maybe start a handmade jewelry business?* The idea seemed outlandish and crazy, but it tugged at my heart.

That afternoon, I drove to a Michaels arts and crafts store down the street from the school where I worked. I walked up and down the rows, trying to find the jewelry section. I finally found it toward the back of the store—an aisle filled with beads, wire, elastic, tools, and other bits and pieces for making jewelry. I wanted to start small, so I picked eight strands of inexpensive glass beads—mostly blues and greens—and a strand of cream-colored freshwater pearls. I found two different sizes of elastic and headed for the checkout lane.

That evening as Steve and I were watching TV, I cut the pre-strung beads from their plastic cords and let them roll around together on a paper plate. I cut an eight-inch length of elastic cord and began to string the beads, one at a time, in a repeating pattern. I tied the ends of the elastic cord together, trimmed them, slid the bracelet onto my wrist, and looked at it—with disappointment. It looked like something made by a child. The beads weren't nearly as beautiful as the ones on the bracelets I had brought home from our trip.

Maybe this was a stupid idea.

I threw the bracelet in the trash and spent the rest of the eve-ning cuddling with Steve on the couch and watching TV.

"Don't get discouraged, babe," he said. "Is there another jewelry store where you can look for better-quality beads?" Steve was always cheering me on, encouraging me to keep trying. When I was quick to give up, he was quick with words of reassurance.

The next morning as I got ready for work, I slipped my boutique bracelets onto my wrist once more and took a good look at them. The colors were natural and rich. The freshwater pearls had a soft sheen; there were small wood beads in a deep brown. I also noticed the small sterling beads added a lot of dimension to these little boutique bracelets. The different textures made them look artisan instead of childish. Before I left for work, I opened the phone book to look for a local bead shop.

Later that day, after I loaded my students on the bus and prepped lessons for the next day, I drove to the bead store, hoping they would have the beautiful beads I wanted. I felt a little intimidated as I walked into the shop. Before me was a whole wall hung with tools I had no idea how to use. I spotted some beautiful shell beads but winced at the price. I moved down the counter a bit and spotted some small aqua beads; they had a milky look to them and were labeled "amazonite." I had no idea what that was, but I loved the look. I picked up a strand and looked at the price—$12. That was way more than I wanted to pay, but I thought perhaps I could use them sparingly and make a few different bracelets with them. I added some round wood beads, bronze freshwater pearls, and sterling silver spacers. I already had elastic cord at home. Then I headed to the register with my carefully chosen strands. The total came to almost $30. I had thought I could re-create my boutique bracelets for a lot less than I paid for them, but so far, my hobby was proving to be pretty expensive.

After dinner that evening, I pulled out another paper plate and again cut the prestrung beads from their cords. One at a time,

I strung them onto elastic in a repeating pattern. Immediately, I could tell that this bracelet was going to be on a whole new level. It was lovely—just as lovely as the bracelets I'd found at the boutique on Coronado. I made four bracelets that evening, using the same beads in various patterns. I loved the way they looked.

The next morning, I slid one of the boutique bracelets onto my wrist and then picked one of my handmade bracelets to wear beside it. I was hooked! But I knew I needed to find a more affordable source for beads and supplies.

The following weekend, my sister and I headed to the beading district in Los Angeles. Oh my goodness, there were more beads than I could have imagined! Street after street, store after store, row after row. And so affordable! I spent $100 and left with a bag full of beads— wood, shell, freshwater pearl, stone, and sterling silver. I could hardly wait to start creating!

That weekend, I made sixteen bracelets. They were just beads strung on stretchy elastic, but they looked so pretty together. I decided to put them in a small basket and take them to the teachers' lounge at work. I put an envelope in the basket that read, "$15 each, or two for $20. Make checks payable to Lisa Leonard."

I arrived at work, set the small basket of bracelets on a table in the lounge, took a deep breath, and headed to my classroom. Much like the elastic cord around my wrist, I was stretching myself by trying something new. It was both exhilarating and unnerving. Bringing my handmade creations into the real world felt risky. I was asking people to pay real money for my bracelets. Allowing other teachers to see my bracelets left me feeling vulnerable—so vulnerable that I almost wanted to crawl under a desk and hide. I reassured myself by reasoning that if none of my bracelets sold, I could give them as gifts to friends.

At lunchtime, I popped into the lounge to find that three

bracelets had sold. One of my colleagues walked by and told me how sweet they were. I smiled a little, hoping she meant the bracelets were sweet—as in dainty and beautiful, not as in silly and childish.

After school, I went to gather my basket of bracelets and found that four more had sold. Seven bracelets sold my first day—not too bad! I exhaled a little. And no one had laughed at me. When I peeked inside the envelope, I saw two checks and a few bills.

Could this maybe, just maybe, be the start of something?

After putting my stretchy bracelets in the teachers' lounge a few more times, I got up the nerve to make a couple of necklaces. I had used crimp beads and nylon wire in high school, so I made a quick trip to Michaels to pick up supplies. The necklaces came together just as beautifully as the bracelets—gorgeous beads strung on wire that were warm and natural with lots of texture. Even better, they sold faster than the bracelets!

It had only been a couple months since I sold my first bracelets and necklaces in the teachers' lounge. Now I was starting to think a little bigger. It would be so nice to put each necklace and bracelet in a drawstring pouch with a business card. There was just one problem: I wasn't a real business.

"Steve, I'm thinking of getting a business license and starting a little jewelry business," I said tentatively. "That way, I can get business cards printed. I'll be more official."

"Go for it, babe!" he said with enthusiasm. "I'm sure you can apply for a business license at city hall."

"Perfect!" I said. "That's what I'll do."

A couple of days later, I found a parking spot near city hall and walked slowly toward the building. I felt an overwhelming sense of dread as I climbed each step.

Are they going to laugh at me? Do they grant business licenses to people like me?

My dad had a small business putting computer systems together. He still worked full-time as a medical technologist, so it was a side hustle—something he did in his spare time. I tried to reassure myself that other people must have small hobby-type businesses, just like my dad—just like I wanted.

Inside city hall, I followed the signs to the small business department. The woman at the front desk handed me an application without looking up from her computer. I filled it out with shaking hands and handed it back to her a few minutes later.

"You should receive your official license in the next seven to ten business days," she said matter-of-factly.

I did it! I applied for a business license and no one laughed at me or asked me questions I couldn't answer. No one called me a fraud!

I went straight over to Staples and picked out business cards from their predesigned selection.

I was officially a business owner, and soon I would have the business cards to prove it!

Be Fully You

There is a place inside your heart
Where you hold your hopes and dreams.
They were planted there by the God of the universe.
They are there for a reason.
They are part of who you are,
Part of who you were made to be.
They matter because you matter.
You being fully you matters.

chapter nineteen

LAUNCHING A JEWELRY BUSINESS

With my new business license in hand, I was officially official. I had sold a few necklaces and bracelets by leaving a basket of jewelry in the teachers' lounge, but I wanted to sell more jewelry and build my business. It was a great place to start. Everyone was supportive and encouraging. Friends and fellow teachers were buying my necklaces. Sometimes a friend of a friend would reach out and ask to see my jewelry. My little business was slowly but surely expanding.

Over the next months and years, I continued to make jewelry. David had already been born, and I was making jewelry—just a side hustle to bring in some extra money and an outlet to express creativity. After Matthias was born, I felt myself ready to stretch even further. I had friends who hosted Pampered Chef parties and Mary Kay makeovers—why not host my own jewelry party? I estimated I would need at least a hundred pieces of jewelry. I would invite friends and women from my church. I would serve cheese and crackers, fresh fruit, and chocolate. It would be a mellow evening of hanging out and trying on jewelry—and it would be the official launch of my business.

I got to work making different kinds of necklaces and bracelets. Each handmade piece was different. I strung beads in the
evening after the boys were in bed, mixing and blending different
colors of stone, glass, pearls, and metal. I wanted each piece to
have its own story, its own unique feel.

A few weeks earlier, I'd made another trip to the beading district in Los Angeles to stock up on supplies. While I was brows-
ing, I saw some beautiful stone pendants in a glass case. Each one
had a wire-wrapped loop so it could be strung onto a necklace.
Those stone pendants looked incredible, with an artisan vibe.

"Can you show me how to wire wrap a pendant?" I asked the
woman behind the counter.

"Sure," she answered as she pulled out a teardrop-shaped
stone, polished to a shiny black finish. "Slip one end of the wire
through the hole and bring the two ends together. Twist this way
and that, and use needle-nose pliers to smooth the ends of the
wire against the metal wrapping." Her experienced hands moved
incredibly fast. I was amazed.

I grabbed a piece of scratch paper and a pen. "Will you show
me one more time," I asked, "more slowly?"

She picked up another stone pendant and cut an eight-inch
length of wire. As she pulled the wire through, twisting and shaping it to form a loop, I sketched the steps so I could remember how
to do it myself. Then I went home and spent the evening practicing. I probably wrapped fifty pendants that evening—twisting
and shaping the wire until my hands started to move with confidence and the wire took on the desired shape.

Now as I created each necklace, I not only strung beads in a
repeating pattern, but I planned the entire design around a stone
pendant. The pendants gave each piece a focal point and the hand-
crafted, artisan feel I wanted. The necklaces looked beautiful.

After brainstorming with my twin sister about how to display the jewelry, I landed on a simple concept. I found shallow metal trays at IKEA for a couple dollars each, and I bought two large bags of white rice at the grocery store. On the afternoon of my first gathering, I put the metal trays on our dining room table and filled them with white rice. Then I laid out the necklaces and bracelets on top of the rice in rows—making sure the colors coordinated and popped in each tray.

The food was prepared and set on a small table off to the side of the dining room. Postcards had been handed out, inviting women to drop by my home between 4 and 7 p.m. Nora Jones was crooning on the CD player; my mom was sitting at a table by the front door to collect cash and checks; and my sister was there for moral support. Steve took the boys out for a few hours so I could focus.

An hour before I was scheduled to greet my first customer, I began to panic.

This is the stupidest idea in the world! What am I going to do with all this jewelry if it doesn't sell? What if no one comes?

I wanted to run away as fast as I could. The whole idea suddenly seemed like a gigantic mistake. It was way too vulnerable, too scary, too much pressure. Each of my handmade pieces felt like an extension of my heart. If the jewelry didn't sell, I was a failure. If the jewelry was no good, perhaps I wasn't any good either.

My mom and sister hugged me and spoke words of encouragement. "The jewelry is beautiful," they said. "Just have fun. We're here to support you."

Soon, two women from church arrived, friends who had been supportive and encouraging as I started my little business. I exhaled. I relaxed a little bit. They walked around the table picking up necklaces, trying them on, and looking into the handheld mirrors set up around the table. After a few minutes, more guests arrived.

Everyone was smiling, talking, and trying on jewelry. Then the first customer went to the table where my mom was sitting to pay for her jewelry. She bought two necklaces and two bracelets. I was shocked and humbled. Women went back and forth, trying on jewelry and asking for my opinion.

Over the course of a few hours, the trays began to empty and the gathering wound down. About forty women had come to the open house, and about half of the jewelry had gone home with them.

As I said good-bye to the last guest and began to tidy up the jewelry, bag the white rice, and stack the metal trays, I looked at my mom, who had been counting checks and cash.

"How much did we sell?" I asked.

"You're not going to believe it," she said. "Just over $700!"

"*What?*" I squealed with delight. "Are you serious?"

It was far beyond anything I had hoped. This was the start of something big; I could feel it.

This Moment

This moment—
I am not where I want to be.
Pacing back and forth,
Waiting and more waiting,
Frustrated,
Side to side,
Sidelined,
Right to left,
I cannot stand still.
Yet I am at a standstill.

I gain no ground.

Planted seeds that will not grow.

This moment—

I am not where I want to be.

Two steps back,

Setback,

Stretched thin,

Discouraged,

I have been here before.

Why am I here again?

I need to learn what I did not learn last time.

A second chance,

A do-over,

A try again.

This moment—

Finally I am where I want to be.

With every side step,

Every back and forth,

Every step back,

Every setback,

I have been preparing.

Scared

But ready

To leap

To bloom

To become.

This moment—

My someday becomes my now.

My maybe becomes my yes.

My what if becomes my what is.

My impossible becomes my plausible.

My inconceivable becomes my feasible.

What I have seen with my heart,

I now see with my eyes.

I step out,

Beyond,

With every seed I have sown,

With every stretch I have grown,

I step bravely into the unknown.

chapter twenty

FRIENDS GATHER

I couldn't believe my first jewelry gathering had been such a success! It boosted my confidence to dream even bigger. A couple of women who came to my first jewelry gathering offered to host gatherings at their homes. It was humbling and empowering to have friends come alongside and support me in my new business.

Over the next year or so, I was able to schedule one or two gatherings every week—and even more gatherings around the holidays. Between November and December, there were weeks when I had gatherings five nights in a row! Steve was incredibly supportive, freeing me up to be gone many evenings and to make jewelry in between.

Lauren, a young woman from our church, was just twelve years old when she started to help care for the boys while I was working. She let herself in the house, checked each boy's diaper, got snacks ready, and pulled out puzzles and games for the boys to play. She knew Matthias's favorite superheroes and how to draw them. She knew David's favorite snack and how to prepare it. She made our lives so much easier! From the time Matthias was four years old, he considered Lauren his best friend. She became part of our family and continued to help with the boys until she got married at twenty-one and moved away. She truly helped raise our boys, and I will forever be grateful for the role she played in our family.

After a few gatherings, I began to get a feel for the amount of jewelry to bring, how long it would take me to set up the displays, and how to collect payments. I wanted to stretch more and decided to approach a couple of local boutiques to see if they would buy my jewelry at wholesale prices for their shops. I started with Hands Gallery—an adorable boutique in San Luis Obispo that carried handmade pottery, housewares, leather journals, and artisan jewelry. I stopped by the shop one day to browse, and before I left, I casually asked a clerk who the buyer was for the store. The owner, Debra, did all the buying.

Perfect!

The next day, I picked a necklace strung with smooth green stones, creamy freshwater pearls, and a gorgeous red stone teardrop pendant. I wrapped it carefully in cream-colored tissue paper and placed it inside an organza drawstring bag. I enclosed a business card and a handwritten note introducing myself and telling Debra I would love to bring my handmade jewelry to her shop for wholesale. I went to the post office with trembling hands, paid for the postage, and sent the box on its way. Then I waited for three days. I figured after three days that the box would have arrived and Debra would have my gift fresh in her mind.

When I called the store and asked to speak with her, the clerk said she wasn't available. That was actually a relief—I was so nervous! I left a message, sat back on the couch, and took a deep breath. *Phew!* I hadn't thought having a business would feel so vulnerable and sometimes downright terrifying! Step by step, I faced each fear.

Later that afternoon, Debra called back. Our conversation

was quick and easy. She was interested in seeing more jewelry! We scheduled a meeting for later in the week.

I carefully chose necklaces and earrings to show her. Each piece was placed in an individual box and gathered to present to Debra. On the day of our meeting, I loaded up my creations, found a parking space near the boutique, and walked with trembling steps into the shop.

Deep breath.

Debra smiled and welcomed me to her shop. We chatted about the beautiful weather outside and a new greeting card line she was carrying. As we stood on either side of the counter and talked, I began to lay out each necklace side by side. I felt like I was laying out my soul, baring some of my most vulnerable hopes and dreams.

She turned her attention to the handmade jewelry in front of her. With the precision of a surgeon and the strong opinions of an experienced buyer, she separated the necklaces into two categories.

Yes.

No.

No.

Yes.

No.

Yes.

With each no, my heart sank a little lower, and I wished the ground would swallow me up. With each yes, my hopes rose slightly. I was on an emotional roller coaster with each response. *She likes it. She hates it. She likes it. She hates it.*

After a few very short minutes—which felt like an eternity— she tallied up the cost for the yes necklaces, pulled out her check- book, and paid me for the pieces. I thanked her, packed up the reject necklaces, walked to my car, drove down the street, pulled into a quiet spot, and burst into tears. I felt humiliated, rejected, and stupid. *Who do I think I am making handmade jewelry? I'm a failure.*

But I could hear a faint voice inside me reminding me of the yeses—that this shop, a shop I loved, was carrying some of my handmade designs. Sure, the owner hadn't liked every piece, but she had liked *some*. Yes, I could make handmade jewelry. I was just starting out, and that was okay. Yes, I could handle rejection and keep moving forward. Yes, I could celebrate my successes, no matter how small.

Love Given Is Love Gained

Bravery makes us stronger.

Smiles are contagious.

Kindness rubs off on others.

Gentleness calms the soul.

Generosity brings freedom.

Creativity inspires creativity

Laughter is infectious.

Honesty breaks down walls.

Forgiveness fortifies the heart.

Love given is love gained.

Good never goes to waste.

It comes back bigger and better.

It grows and stretches and

Binds us together.

chapter twenty-one

BUILDING LISA LEONARD DESIGNS TOGETHER

By 2006, I was hosting one or two home gatherings a week and had about fifteen boutiques that carried my designs. I wanted to try something new to see if the business could grow. So I started blogging and set a goal of growing my website visits to one hundred people a day. My daily posts were short and simple—a few pictures with short captions to talk about our family, our life with two toddlers, David's disability, and DIY ideas for decorating and entertaining. Occasionally, I shared a picture of a recent necklace I created. Blogging was an incredible way to connect with other moms, and I loved it.

Not long after I started the blog, I was reading a DIY jewelry magazine that featured a detailed article on how to create a pet tag by using metal stamps. As I read the article, I thought, *Moms would love a necklace with their child's name on it!* I kept reading, trying to understand exactly how handstamping worked. I wanted to elevate this idea from pet tags to beautiful jewelry created just for moms.

At the end of the article, a number of resources were listed. I immediately looked up every website and wrote down all the supplies I'd need to create a handstamped necklace. I ordered the items on my list, and they arrived in our mailbox within a week. I couldn't wait to get started! I organized the stamps in alphabetical order and sorted the metal blanks that would become pendants. I found a hammer in the garage and placed a piece of wood on our kitchen countertop. I carefully lined up the steel stamp on the metal blank and hit it with my hammer as hard as I could. When I raised the stamp to see the impression it left behind, I saw a letter that was faint and crooked.

Okay, I'm going to need more practice.

I took a deep breath and tried again, this time hitting the steel stamp as hard as I could. Then I hit it a second time for good measure. The impression was slightly better—a bit less crooked, but still too faint. After trying and mostly failing for a half hour or so, I gave up. *Handstamping is stupid,* I thought. I threw the supplies in a box, put them in the garage, and spent the evening next to Steve on the couch. We watched a movie while I created three beaded necklaces.

The next day, I woke up with renewed determination.

There has to be a way to get the impression clearer. Each letter on the pet tag was clear and crisp. What am I doing wrong?

I went back to the magazine and reread the steps. From what I could see, I had done everything correctly, but my result looked nothing like the pictures in the article. I noticed the author's bio included his contact information. *Should I email him? Would he respond to a random reader making jewelry in her home?*

I took a deep breath and ran to my computer before I could lose my nerve. I sent him a short email thanking him for the article, describing my problem, and asking for additional tips.

I couldn't believe it when he emailed me back just two hours later! His kindness was a gentle nudge pushing me forward and encouraging me to keep trying.

"Did you lay your metal blank on a solid steel block?" he asked. "You'll get a clear impression when you use a steel block on a solid surface."

It made sense! The list of supplies included a steel block, but I hadn't known what it was for, so I had skipped over it. I Googled "steel block" and found a website that carried them. They were small and very heavy, and they cost around $40. According to the author, this was the tool I needed. A stranger had taken time to help me and give me advice. We didn't know each other, but I trusted him. The steel block was a splurge, but I ordered it immediately.

After my solid steel block arrived, I tried the whole process again. I laid the block on our kitchen counter, lined up the steel stamp on the metal blank, and hit it with my hammer as hard as I could. This time the stamped letter was still a bit crooked, but it was nice and clear. *Maybe this handstamping thing isn't so stupid after all!*

In early 2007, I shared my first handstamped necklace design on the blog. It was a simple round disk with the word *LOVE* stamped across it in capital letters. *Love*—a little word with so much power. Seeing *LOVE* on the pendant moved me. It represented my heart, so full of love for my two little boys. It represented our marriage and the commitment Steve and I had to each other. It represented my desire to bring more love and more beauty to the world. Words held so much meaning. I wanted to make necklaces that held deep meaning. I wanted to make jewelry that represented what mattered most—jewelry that represented the love of family and the hope that resides in each of us.

A week later, one of my friends hosted a home gathering for me. There were about twenty women there, mingling, munching on snacks, and looking at jewelry. Steve came with the boys to help me set up the displays before the gathering and to help clean up at the end of the evening. We mixed in a few handstamped necklaces with all my beaded designs. The women at the gathering loved the new pieces! They wanted personalized necklaces with their children's names stamped on them. That evening, Steve caught my eye and smiled. He knew there was something special about handstamped jewelry. He was encouraging me to keep going.

Within a couple months, my beaded necklaces stopped selling altogether. The handstamped necklaces and bracelets were the only things selling at my home gatherings. The local boutiques that carried my jewelry wanted handstamped designs too. I had always loved making beaded necklaces, each one put together with different colors and textures. A necklace could change the entire look of an outfit. But I could feel something big and important happening with handstamped jewelry. Instead of just changing the look of an outfit, handstamped jewelry can serve as a reminder of what matters most. Instead of reflecting beauty on the outside, handstamped jewelry can reflect the beauty of the heart.

My hobby business started with home gatherings and small wholesale accounts at neighborhood boutiques, but it was growing beyond our local community. Within a year of writing my first post, I had more than one thousand people reading my blog—far beyond my initial goal. I couldn't believe it! *One thousand people read my blog every day? Who are these women?*

I imagined walking around a room filled with one thousand women. They were moms, wives, sisters, daughters—people just like me. They worked hard and put their family's needs before their own. They kissed their toddlers' sticky faces and prayed that naptime would go smoothly, just like I did. I wondered if they also felt as tired as I did. *Do they feel like a failure when they lose their temper and scream at their children, like I do? Do they crave ten minutes alone in the bathroom, like I do? Do they collapse in exhaustion at the end of the day, like I do?*

When I shared my handstamped designs on the blog, the strong response caught me by surprise. Readers immediately asked how they could buy these personalized necklaces and bracelets online. They were supportive, cheering me on and sharing words of encouragement.

Okay, so how do I take orders online?

I decided to put together a simple blog post with eight different necklace designs, along with a brief description and the price for each design. In the post, I included instructions for how to email me to place an order. From there, I began to correspond with my readers directly, sending PayPal links back and forth and handwriting custom order slips. It was extremely labor-intensive and low-tech, but it worked! On the front end, at least.

Behind the scenes was a different story. Piles of paper were strewn across our kitchen table and counters, and metal stamps, hammers, and chains were everywhere. We couldn't eat dinner at our kitchen table without spending thirty minutes clearing jewelry supplies and customer orders. As the online community continued to grow and orders kept coming in, Steve had an idea.

"You know, babe," he said, "if we build you a website, it can handle all of this paperwork for you."

"How would I process payments?" I asked.

"The website would have a system for processing orders and taking payments," he explained. "You wouldn't have to do it manually anymore."

I imagined the relief of not having to send PayPal links to every customer. I imagined a system that organized orders for me. It sounded good. I felt the excitement, but I also felt nervous. *Can we really do this?*

Steve quickly jumped into action. He enlisted the help of one of his college students from church, Ryan, who was working on a degree in software engineering, and they began to build a website, complete with beautiful pictures, clear product descriptions, and text boxes where customers could enter their customization. They set up the website to process payments as well. They worked tirelessly every evening for months, writing code, designing each page, and laying a path to guide the customers through the ordering process.

When the guys launched the new website three months later, it transformed the business. I suddenly had one-tenth of the emails to answer each day. No more handwriting each order, no more sending PayPal links back and forth, no more paper cluttering the kitchen counter. Now I could go into the back end of the website and print orders, which meant less human error. It was a game changer for Lisa Leonard Designs.

The website made things run much more efficiently. Now I had more time to design and make jewelry—to do the things I really loved—and that brought me joy. I started reaching out to other bloggers, asking if I could send them one of my custom necklaces in exchange for a post on their blog. I would handstamp a custom necklace just for them, and they could share it with their blog community.

This was back in the days when blog marketing was very grassroots. There were no big businesses using blogs to market. It was mostly just mamas who wanted to connect and share their lives, handmade products, and creative ideas. I had a long list of blogs I read daily. I loved scrapbooking blogs, decorating blogs, DIY blogs, and photography blogs. I reached out to each blogger individually to share my jewelry and connect with them. Once again, I felt vulnerable as I put myself out there, not only sharing my designs (and my heart!) but also asking for something in return. *Will they laugh at me? Will they think I'm ridiculous?*

I carefully typed each email. I watched for typos and tried to be clear and confident. With trembling fingers, I hit "send" and waited nervously for a response. Then incredible things began to happen. These amazing mamas were saying yes! Women I respected and admired wanted to wear my jewelry and share it with their communities. It was humbling and so very exciting.

Not everyone said yes, but no one laughed at me. Most of them wanted to support my business. I am still thankful for these women. They took a chance on me. They believed in me. They gave me courage to dream even bigger. Having the support of the blogging community and Steve by my side gave me even more courage to risk and to grow.

While the back end of the business was now a more efficient engine, I was still working from our kitchen table—handstamping personalized necklaces one at a time. While I stayed busy making jewelry and answering customer emails, my friend Cara helped me out by packing and shipping orders. Every day, she brought her baby over, and we let the kids play while we worked. It was awesome and chaotic. I was making about fifty necklaces a week at that time—plenty to keep both me and Cara busy while Steve and Ryan made sure the technical side of the business worked well.

After Christmas in 2009, about two years after selling my first handstamped designs, I got an email from *Parenting* magazine asking if they could feature my jewelry in their May issue. "Sure!" I said, and I mailed them a couple of personalized necklaces. Then I promptly forgot all about it.

A few months later, in April, I woke up early one morning and opened my email to see how many order notifications had come through while I was asleep. It was part of my morning routine. Usually there were around five to ten notifications. I would print out all the new orders so I would be ready when Cara arrived. But on this morning, there were more notifications than usual. I went through line by line, counting the number of new order emails— and there were twenty-six! *What? Is there a glitch in the website? Am I getting multiple notifications for each order?*

I went to the back end of the website to investigate. Every single order had a different purchaser. Each order was original—I wasn't receiving multiple notifications! I began printing orders and saw that almost every order was for the Captured Heart necklace—one of the necklaces I had sent to the editor of *Parenting* magazine. *The May issue must be out!*

I called Steve at work. "Babe, I'm freaking out! We have twenty-six new orders this morning! I think the *Parenting* magazine article just came out."

"Wow, sweetie, that's awesome!" he said. "You might want to order more supplies. I'm sure more orders will come in over the next few days."

He was so smart! I hadn't even thought about that. I went to the wholesale website and stocked up on the various materials I needed to make the necklaces—sterling silver blanks, chain, and soldering paste.

Once the boys were up, dressed, and fed, we headed to the grocery store to buy a copy of the magazine. We pulled into the parking lot, and I quickly unbuckled the kids from their car seats and buckled them directly into the double stroller. We went inside the store and headed straight for the magazine aisle.

My eyes scanned over the magazines—past the decorating magazines, past the cooking magazines, and straight to the parenting section. *There it is!* I picked up the May issue and flipped through page by page until I saw a photo of the Captured Heart necklace. There it was in print—a full page, with my name and website at the bottom of the page! I could hardly believe it. I would have stood there stunned for a few minutes longer, but I had two toddlers trying to climb out of their double stroller. I scooped up a few more copies of the magazine to share with my mom and sisters, grabbed some necessary groceries, and got through the checkout line as quickly as I could.

I returned home with the boys, put everything away, and got the boys their midmorning snack. Once they were happily playing, I went over to my computer again. Another fifteen orders had come through while we were at the grocery store. By the time Steve got home from work that evening, we were up to eighty-five orders—by far my biggest day ever!

I was on a high! And I was moving fast and furious to keep up. I had to create as many Captured Heart necklaces as I could, return customer emails, make sure the boys were taken care of, and obsessively check to see how many new orders were coming in. That week, we went from the usual fifty orders to almost eight hundred orders!

Four days after the *Parenting* magazine article came out, I started to get worried and a little tired. Orders continued to pour in, with no signs of slowing down. I had been working until midnight each night and then waking up early with the boys. We had Lauren, now thirteen, helping take care of the boys. She was homeschooled, and so she had some free time during the day.

My kindergarten
school picture. 1979

Steve with his dog Saul. 1977

Steve and me enjoying lunch out
while we were dating in 1999.

Ready to get married.
July 24, 1999.

The bouquet and bouton-
niere my friends made
for us. July 24, 1999

Just after we said our vows. July 24, 1999

Shopping to prepare for baby David.
I'm about six months pregnant. April 2002

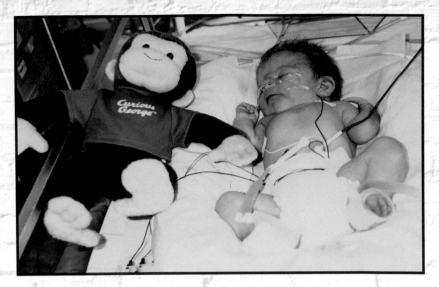

David on the day of his birth. July 4, 2002

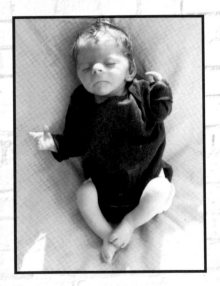

David the day after he was released from the NICU, just three weeks old and about five pounds. July 2002

David at three months old. He had just been released from his second stay in the hospital. October 2002

Matthias right after he was released from the hospital. About one week old. January 2004

Steve cuddles Matthias. May 2004

Our little family of four. Matthias is about three months; David is about twenty-one months. April 2004

Two squirmy babies.
May 2004

A sunny day at the
park when the boys
were toddlers. 2007

Superhero Matthias—
potholders, rain boots,
and a blankie cape.
2006

The first handstamped
necklace I made.
Early 2007

The stacking rings are
one of my favorite pieces—
simple and organic and
perfect for every day.

Hanging out with some of my sisters—twin sis,
Chrissie, and my two younger sisters (also twins),
Susan and Ellen. We all have August birthdays, and
each summer we get away together. August 2015

A family day in Cayucos, California. David is nine years old; Matthias is eight years old. June 2012

Family photo. December 2017

She was a lifesaver! Cara was working extra hours to pack and ship twice the number of orders she usually did. We were all working as hard as we could, but we were barely making a dent in fulfilling the incoming orders.

Steve jumped in with a new strategy.

"Lisa, there is no way you and Cara can do this on your own," he said. "We need to bring in more people and get an assembly line set up. We can train college students and move things along much faster."

"There's no time," I said, on the verge of tears. "We just have to work harder and get through this crazy season until things slow down."

"What if things don't slow down?" he asked. "What if you get another magazine feature and things stay busy? You can't grow a business this way. You need a team. We need to train more people. Please let me help you."

"Okay," I said, unsure of how things would work. "Will you help me get a team of people trained?"

Steve jumped in, and thank God he did! I was crumbling like a stale chocolate chip cookie. Honestly, I was ready to pull the plug, shut down the website, and stop blogging. I was tired and couldn't see the way forward. But Steve had a vision. He knew just what we needed to take our little business through this growing season and into the next one.

From the beginning, Steve encouraged and supported me, but now he was regularly involved with Lisa Leonard Designs. We were a team. What started as *my* hobby business was now a business we worked in *together*. The business needed him as much as it needed me. He was the adult ministries pastor at our church, which included overseeing the college ministry. He had a group of awesome college students ready to jump in and help with the flood of incoming orders. He scheduled them, trained them, and set up systems to make the process faster and more efficient.

Once the rush from the *Parenting* magazine article subsided, we put our heads together to strategize how to reinvest those dollars into the business. Steve talked with a friend, who agreed to sublet us part of his building, and so we moved the business out of our home and into a real workspace. Steve interviewed bankers, lawyers, insurance brokers, and bookkeepers. We hired a manager, one of the college students who had stood out and taken initiative. Steve made everyone official employees instead of independent contractors. We trained people on all the various parts of the business—from stamping and assembly to customer service and shipping.

Steve had a vision to grow the business and make it successful. He set up our corporate structure, bank accounts, bookkeeping system, marketing strategy, employee manual, and a consulting relationship—all the things that had never crossed my mind. It was crazy fun to watch the business grow. Steve could see what I couldn't see. I had creative ideas for jewelry and loved blogging, but Steve could see the bigger business picture. What scared me was exactly what excited him!

When we started working together, I was tempted to say Steve was the brains and I was the heart. But Steve had so much heart and I had a lot of brains. We both had brains and heart. It was our combination of brains and heart that made things work so well. Together, we were more creative and more insightful and could do bigger things. We made a great team. Of course, we sometimes got frustrated and drove each other crazy. There were times we yelled at each other in front of our employees. It was imperfect because we were imperfect and because we were on such a steep and speedy learning curve. But there was no denying it—our strengths were well matched.

It wouldn't be long before our business would need a real CEO. Steve and I debated if we should hire someone to come in and help us grow or if he should quit his job as a pastor and take over as CEO. After a year of spending his days off and evenings on the business, we made the big leap. Steve left his job as a pastor and jumped into running Lisa Leonard Designs full-time. It was one of the scariest and best decisions we've ever made!

Growing the business meant we spent our days together at the office, working and planning. Steve was now officially the CEO, and his brilliant mind began to build this dream, to carry out this vision. I continued designing jewelry and connecting with our community on social media. When the business was doing well, we celebrated. *We're a success! Nothing can stop us.* When the business was struggling, we were stressed and worried. *Can we handle this? Maybe we should both just go out and get regular jobs.*

We hired employees and fired employees, hired marketing firms and fired marketing firms, had busy seasons and had slow seasons. We had big ups and big downs. As we grew, we relocated multiple times, making space for more employees and more supplies. We made small mistakes, and we made big mistakes, and we tried to learn from all of them.

Steve and I were creative thinkers, willing to risk and to try hard things. Steve loved to learn and seemed to thrive best in the most challenging times. When I was ready to give up, he was ready to push forward. Together, we strategized and tried to think outside the box. Despite the challenges, our little business grew every year. We were building Lisa Leonard Designs together and dreaming up new ideas and brands. Steve's vision didn't stop there. Lisa Leonard Designs was just the beginning.

How to Think Good Thoughts

1. **Hold it in your hand.**

   How does it feel? Too heavy? Too sharp? Is it dangerous? Is it true?

   Put it back. This thought isn't for you.

   But if it has a nice texture, like a smooth seashell, move on to step 2.

2. **Try it on for size.**

   How does it fit? Too tight? Too scratchy? Does it pull and tug?

   Put it back. This thought isn't for you.

   But if it fits well, like a good pair of broken-in blue jeans, move on to step 3.

3. **Take it into your heart.**

   This is a good thought. It is beautiful and true.

   Keep it with you at all times.

   Let it make itself at home inside you.

   Soon it will become part of you, part of the sunshine that is your soul.

chapter twenty-two

INSPIRATION
AND IMITATION

One of the hardest parts of owning our own business and designing jewelry is seeing my designs copied by another artist. I love to support other small business owners, and I believe the market is big enough for every artist to share their creations with the world. I've met amazing women who design handmade treasures that move my heart and bring beauty to the world, and I love being inspired by them. Together, we are part of a creative community. I am grateful to them for who they are and what they bring to the world. Their work is an inspiration to me, and mine can be an inspiration to them. *Inspiration* is an incredible thing, but *imitation* is something else entirely.

Inspiration brings energy; imitation saps energy.

Inspiration multiplies creativity; imitation diminishes creativity.

Inspiration gives joy; imitation causes pain.

A few months after I started making handstamped jewelry and sharing it on my blog, another blogger started making handstamped jewelry. That didn't bother me—I had met many bloggers who've launched handstamped jewelry businesses, and we had a mutual respect and friendship. There is space for every artist.

The problem with this handstamped jeweler (let's call her Cindy) was that she didn't design her own jewelry—she took designs, sometimes from me and sometimes from other artists. She copied other people's designs and called them her own. Not only were her designs similar to mine, but Cindy also named her pieces the same names as mine and sometimes even copied my product descriptions. She photographed the jewelry in the same style I used to photograph my designs. It was blatant imitation.

Any artist who has shared their creations with the world has encountered copycats. It's part of the way life works. With admiration comes inspiration and, unfortunately, imitation. I was thrilled when my jewelry started to sell and my business grew, but when I saw my designs being imitated, I was angry.

I wish I could say that Cindy was a minor annoyance or that the anger I felt came and then quickly dissipated, but that wasn't the case. I was angry—really, really angry. Angry with a capital A. I was so angry that there were times I wanted to stop making jewelry and stop sharing my designs with the world. It was too painful. Sometimes I hated Cindy. I hated her in a way I had never hated anyone else in my whole life.

I had spent hours dreaming, playing, sketching, molding, and metalworking to breathe life into every new design. I had spent even more hours crafting words to share my heart behind each piece. I wanted my community to know what each necklace, each ring, and each bracelet meant to me. I wanted them to hear my heart and to find inspiration and connection. But every time I shared a new design, it wasn't long until Cindy took that design, changed it slightly, and called it her own. I felt wronged, angry, and hateful. It's embarrassing to put those feelings in print, but it's true. I complained to my husband and close friends, but mostly I held on to the anger and ugliness.

Steve and I had copyrighted all of our designs, and we consulted a lawyer at one point to see if we should pursue a lawsuit. In the end, we learned it is very hard for artists to protect their designs. We were given good advice to take the energy we would have spent on a court battle and devote it to coming up with new designs and building our business. So we did.

Instead of looking back, we looked forward. We worked harder and thought outside the box. We went all out to continually grow and change and be more creative. I took jewelry classes to learn new skills and expand my knowledge base. I tried to stop worrying about what Cindy was doing and to focus instead on building a community and reaching more people. We were doing great. The business was growing, but in my heart, I still felt angry.

Then one day, I had an idea. I realized that I had spent a tremendous amount of time thinking about how hurtful it was that Cindy had taken my designs, but I had never told Cindy how I felt. I had never asked her to stop. I had never engaged with her and spoken my truth. *Should I call her and tell her how I feel?* Just thinking about calling her made my heart race. It was a crazy idea. I was so nervous to speak with her, but I had been angry for so long.

I had just finished buying groceries. All the bags were loaded into the trunk, and as I climbed into the driver's seat, I decided it was now or never. I was alone, and I had a few minutes—I should just go for it. I looked up her website and found her contact information. Then I called her office and asked to speak with her.

"Hello," said the person who answered the phone.

My heart was beating fast in my chest.

"Hello," I said, "is Cindy available?"

"Yes, may I ask who's calling?"

"This is Lisa Leonard," I said, my voice shaking.

Dang it! I wished I could be calm, cool, and collected.

I was placed on hold and could practically hear my heart beating in my chest while I waited.

"Hello, this is Cindy."

"Hi, Cindy, this is Lisa Leonard. Do you have a couple minutes to chat?"

There was a slight pause, an awkward silence, and then she said, "Sure. What's up?"

She sounded calm, cool, and collected. She sounded like I wished I sounded.

"Well," I began, wishing my voice would stop shaking, "over the last couple of years, I've seen you take my designs and call them your own. I would like to ask you to please stop stealing my designs."

Another pause. Thoughts ran fast through my head. *Oh my gosh! Am I really doing this? Am I really speaking to Cindy on the phone and asking her to stop stealing my designs?*

Then she laughed. "Lisa, I have no idea what you're talking about. Do you really think I have time to look at your designs and copy them?"

I hadn't expected that response. I don't know what I expected, but it wasn't that. She sounded so confident—she even had a mocking tone in her voice. *Am I crazy?* I took a breath and regrouped.

"I don't know what your schedule looks like," I said, "but over and over, you have taken my designs, my words, and even my photography style and called them your own."

"Can you give me some specific examples?" she said, with no trace of nervousness or worry.

"We could go over various pieces one at a time," I said, "but you know what I'm talking about."

"No," she responded, "I have no idea what you're talking about. Is there anything else?"

I was getting nowhere. I took another deep breath.

"Just one more thing," I said. "You don't have to admit anything to me, but every day you have to look at yourself in the mirror. You know what you've done. I'll ask you again, please stop copying my designs."

"Okay, well, thanks," she said.

And we hung up.

I was shaking. *I can't believe I got up the nerve to call her. I can't believe I told her what I thought. I can't believe she sounded so confident. I can't believe she denied the whole thing!*

I sat in my car, phone still in my hand, trying to calm down. After a few minutes, my heart stopped beating so fast and my breathing returned to normal. Then something unexpected happened—I felt *so much better!* I didn't feel angry. I didn't hate her. I felt *fine*. I felt peaceful. The spell was broken! Nothing about the situation changed, but *I changed*. I spoke my truth. Instead of hiding and harboring anger, I showed up and spoke up—and it changed the whole situation for me. I no longer felt powerless.

For the first time, I saw how speaking my truth, telling someone my honest thoughts and opinions, could change things. Speaking my truth didn't change everything, but it changed me. It was a scary but empowering discovery. I had a brand-new tool in my toolbox—showing up and being honest. It was a skill I wanted to practice until I got really good at it—not just in business, but in every area of my life.

A Life Well Lived

There are wins and losses.

There are triumphs and sorrows.

There are moments when everything aligns and runs smoothly.

But most of the time, the to-do lists are long and unfinished at the end of the day.

What's working? Do more of that.

What's not working? Do less of that.

Admit you're not perfect.

Forgive yourself.

Forgive others.

Throw yourself into loving with your whole heart, and don't forget to love your own heart too.

In moments of sadness, find a quiet spot where tears can flow.

In moments of happiness, belly laugh without apology.

When anger courses through your veins, don't push it down. Look it in the eye. Let it out with screams and shouts. Then let it go.

Take time for reflection. Time to be and not to do. Time for quiet.

Live in the moment, refusing to dwell on the past, refusing to worry about the future.

Be brave; speak your truth.

Let it be messy; let it be beautiful.

Soak it up.

This is a life well lived.

chapter twenty-three

THE PERFECT
BERRY CRUMBLE

Every marriage goes through hard times, and about fifteen years into ours, Steve and I were in one of those times. We had already worked through difficult things in our marriage. We had weathered losing a job, seeing some of our closest friends divorce, having a baby with special needs, bringing home another baby just eighteen months later, and starting a business together, with all the craziness it entails. But now we were faced with something new. We simply weren't connecting.

No matter how hard I tried, I couldn't make him happy. He tried hard too, but we could not see eye to eye. We were both hurting, but we didn't know how to help each other. We were both making mistakes, but we didn't know what they were.

During this time, we had plans to gather with friends for a celebration. I decided to make Steve's favorite dessert—berry crumble. This was not going to be just any berry crumble; I was going to make the *perfect* berry crumble. I wanted to show Steve how much I loved him. I wanted to show him he was precious to me. I wanted to make him happy. This berry crumble was going to knock his socks off.

I spent time researching online to find the best recipe. I gathered all the ingredients and spent a good chunk of the day making
the amazing dessert. As the celebration approached, I slowly
pulled the hot crumble out of the oven and gently wrapped it in a
heavy towel before we all hopped into the car. We parked in front
of our friends' home, and I got out carefully, maneuvering the hot
berry crumble to avoid a spill. I took a few steps but then suddenly
lost hold of the wrapped glass dish. I watched in slow-motion
horror as my perfect crumble shattered and splattered all over the
sidewalk. I felt the sting of hot tears behind my eyes.

Hold it together. Hold it together. Hold it together!

But I couldn't hold it together. I'd been trying to hold it
together for so long. The tears overflowed, and once they started,
they would not stop. I could barely catch my breath between sobs.
This was no ordinary berry crumble; this was the *perfect* berry
crumble. This crumble was going to show Steve how much I cared
for him. This dessert was going to save our marriage. It was going
to make Steve fall in love with me again. I looked down at the
berry crumble splattered all over the sidewalk and sobbed.

For years, I tried so hard to be good enough. I tried to be the
perfect wife. I tried to become less so he could be more. Instead,
I became less than whole—and a relationship can't thrive without
two whole people. I thought being perfect would bring me joy. But
I was so focused on being perfect that I was missing all the joy.

I'd spent most of my life believing that if I could be perfect,
or at least almost perfect, I would be good enough. I would be
lovable. So I worked hard to create the perfect life for us. I tried
to create a beautiful, tidy home. I tried to be the perfect mother—
patient and fun and consistent. I tried to be happy even when I
felt sad. I tried to be needless and wantless so I could take care of
everybody else's needs and wants.

With four people in our family and so many differing opinions, things got complicated. I thought I could make things less complicated by being what I considered flexible and easygoing. Instead of saying what I needed and wanted, I would just go with the flow. If I went with the flow, that meant less conflict, and less conflict meant we would all be happier.

But it wasn't working.

Pushing my needs and wants aside did not make them go away—they were all still there, just under the surface. Ignoring them only made me feel more agitated and frustrated. So I tried to ignore *those* feelings as well—and sometimes I seemed to succeed, but other times, I exploded with anger. All the things I needed and wanted, all the things I was feeling but was ignoring, had to find a way out.

In reality, my good intentions to take care of everybody simply cloaked my need to be controlling—to feel that I had value because my life and my relationships were perfectly under control. If I could manage everything and everyone, if there were no unmet needs and no conflict, I believed I would at last feel good enough. I was scared that I wasn't lovable, so I tried to control everything and everyone I could. And yet here we were. The more I tried to control Steve, our marriage, and our family, the more out of control I felt. I had worked tirelessly to try to hold it all together, but we were a mess—as shattered and splattered as the berry crumble.

For so many years, I had been stumbling around trying to be perfect and wondering why I was so unhappy. Now I was beginning to see things more clearly.

There are four people in our family, and I am one of them.

There are two people in our marriage, and I am one of them.

I am a person—a whole person with needs and wants and feelings and ideas.

Just like David has needs—to make music on his keyboard, to be bathed, to eat blended foods, to cuddle in close, to read books together—I have needs as well.

Just like Matthias has needs—to have pencils and paper with him when we leave the house, to have a good book to read, to cuddle with his pugs, to have alone time to recharge—I have needs as well.

Just like Steve has needs—to work out regularly, to play his guitar, to stretch himself, to learn new things and grow, to see his friends and laugh—I have needs as well.

My needs were no less important than the needs of anyone else in our family. My needs were *just as important* as everyone else's needs. To be a whole person, I was going to have to make some big changes. Perhaps most importantly, I had to figure out what I needed and wanted. I had to figure out what I thought and felt.

Ignoring my needs and wants had not helped my family or me. Now, instead of perfection, I wanted wholeness. I wanted to be a whole person. I wanted to take care of myself so I could take care of my family without trying to control them. I wanted them to know who I was—what I wanted and needed—so they could take care of me. I wanted to be authentic instead of trying to live up to the perfectionistic ideals of who I thought I was supposed to be.

Honesty looked like me showing up and being my truest self. It looked like Steve showing up and being his truest self. It was going to take a lot more than the perfect berry crumble to fix this marriage. Marriage requires two people to show up and be honest with each other.

Honesty is imperfect and messy, but it is real. Sometimes it is more than messy; it is ugly and dark and scary. I did not like messy. I had been trying to make my marriage work without actually showing up and being a whole person. I thought if I could make Steve happy, he would love me—but he already loved me. He loved *me*. He wanted me to be *me*. Instead, I was being less than myself to avoid conflict. I wanted our relationship to be nice and tidy, but I was learning that "nice and tidy" is not how healthy relationships work. Life is messy; marriage is messy; kids are messy; and friendships are messy.

When I showed up in the mess and was open, I took a step toward Steve.

When I shared my honest thoughts and desires, I let Steve see me and know me.

It was only when both of us were brave and real that our hearts connected.

When our hearts connected, we began to discover joy.

I couldn't control my husband or my kids. I couldn't keep our home perfectly clean.

I was not perfect. I was just me.

I wanted to be loved for who I was—my truest self. I wanted to be in an honest marriage, where we stepped into the mess together, and together we worked to make something beautiful. I wanted to let my kids be kids—in all their moods and messes and silliness. I wanted to order pizza instead of stressing about making the perfect meal. I wanted to see the toys and shoes all over the family room not as a mess, but as evidence of living a full life together. I wanted to let go of perfect and embrace truth. I wanted to be present in the crazy ups and downs of everyday life.

I wanted all these things, but they seemed so far out of reach. I was learning I had to let go of perfection to have joy. I was learning I had to show up and speak up and be honest—no matter how messy. I was learning it was the only way for us to have a marriage in which we connected and truly knew each other. I was learning the only way to give and receive love is to be completely me— nothing more, nothing less.

But what did it mean to be *me*?

You Are Enough

When you're imperfect,

You are enough.

When you're on top of the world,

You are enough.

When you feel confident,

You are enough.

When you feel small,

You are enough.

When you're weak,

You are enough.

When you cross off every item on your to-do list,

You are enough.

When you curl up in your bed and cry,

You are enough.

When you order pizza for the third night in a row,

You are enough.

When you laugh with friends,

You are enough.

When you have a good hair day,

You are enough.

When you go to the grocery store in sweats,

You are enough.

When you scream in frustration,

You are enough.

When you roll with the punches,

You are enough.

When you get tragically behind on email,

You are enough.

When you try to succeed,

You are enough.

When you're late to pick up your kid,

You are enough.

When everything is going well,

You are enough.

When everything is falling apart,

You are enough.

No matter what you feel or how you look,

Whether you succeed or whether you fail,

You are enough,

Right now, just as you are.

You are created to be *you* in all your amazing imperfection.

The God of the universe loves you and says,

"You are enough."

chapter twenty-four

MEETING JAZMIN

A few months later, on a typical summer day in central
California—warm with blue skies and bright sunshine—
Steve and I were working hard on our business and our marriage.
We were in couples counseling, learning how to love each other
and ourselves more fully. It was a bumpy road with ups and
downs.

On the day before my forty-first birthday, I had a phone call
planned with Bri McKoy, a staffer with Compassion International.
Compassion is an incredible organization, a champion of using
child sponsorship to change lives, change families, and change
communities. Bri has led trips for bloggers and other influencers
all over the world so they can see firsthand what Compassion
does to help children in poverty. Steve and I had been talking for
a few months about going with Compassion to the Dominican
Republic, and Bri and I had set up a phone appointment to discuss details.

Steve and I had a big heart for the Dominican Republic. We
worked with jewelry artisans there, and we loved the beauty of
the country. But privately, I was a little nervous about taking a
trip with Compassion. I had spoken with other bloggers who had

life-changing experiences on these trips with Compassion. *Am I
up for a life-changing experience?*

When Steve and I traveled internationally for business, we
usually saw the touristy side of the countries we visited—the
clean beaches and nice restaurants. I knew this trip would take
us to very different parts of the DR. We would see poverty. We
would visit people who often lived without electricity, clean water,
or sufficient food. I loved the DR, but I was afraid that my heart
couldn't take the pain of seeing the suffering side of the country.

Bri and I had an easy conversation. She was upbeat and smart,
and I liked her immediately. She told me about the other bloggers
who were going on the trip and described what our time in the
DR would be like. We would stay at an American hotel. Our food
would be cooked by people who knew how Americans eat. During
the day, we'd take a bus to different villages to see the Compassion
programs firsthand and visit the homes of families served by
Compassion.

It all sounded good, easy even. I loved the DR; I loved adventure; and I loved seeing new places and meeting new people.
My mind was made up.

*We'll go. It will be good to see the DR from a different perspec-
tive. But I will protect my heart. I won't feel too much. I won't let
the poverty break me. I won't cry. I'll be strong.*

Steve and I arrived in the DR a day before the rest of the team
on February 14, 2015. It was Valentine's Day, so with a recommen-
dation from the hotel concierge, we ventured down the street to a
lovely Italian restaurant. It was nice to have a relaxing evening,
with time to talk about and process how we had started the day in
California and ended it in a balmy, bustling city in the Dominican
Republic. We were thankful to get a good night's sleep before
meeting up with our team the following day.

Early the next morning, we joined our group right outside the hotel. Together, we boarded a white bus with turquoise velvet curtains in each window. Each curtain was edged with turquoise pom-poms. The bus was awesome, especially the velvet curtains on each window. The entire city seemed to be bursting with color—from the happy curtains in our bus to the brightly painted buildings to the brilliant sun overhead. We rode that bus every day to visit different villages and meet different children. That bus drove us past tall palm trees and lush jungles.

We spent the first couple days of our trip getting to know our team members, adjusting to the time change, and visiting Compassion programs. We sang songs and quickly picked up the hand motions and dance moves for each one. We hugged kids and got to know the adults from the local churches who pour their lives into these children. We jumped in and found ourselves accepted and welcomed into each community we visited.

On the third day of our trip, we climbed into the white bus with velvet curtains and drove to a small village outside the city. We attended a morning program that reminded me of the vacation Bible school programs I attended as a kid. We sang songs with the kids, did crafts, and had a snack. During the craft time, I smiled at a little girl across the room, and she came over to me. She shyly moved close to me, and I put my arm around her and gave her a little squeeze. She was adorable. I didn't speak much Spanish, so I reached into my bag and pulled out a pad of white construction paper and a pen, hoping I could think of some way to connect with her.

"What's your name?" I asked her. She told me her name and then wrote it down for me. I looked at what she wrote, and then I drew her name again, using big block letters across the white paper. I handed her the paper.

"Would you like to color this?" I asked.

Her face lit up. There were crayons on the table, and she quickly got to work, carefully coloring in each letter.

There was an older girl nearby, and she asked me in Spanish to write her name in block letters. She wrote her name for me, and again I drew big block letters, filling up the page with her name. As I finished, I looked up to see that five other children had gathered around, each one hoping to have their name written in big block letters.

So I got to work. I drew as fast as I could, and every time I finished a name, more children had gathered. I drew and drew until our time was over and the kids had returned to the meeting area for their next activity.

I got up from the table, thankful that I had found a way to connect with so many children. There was something really special about each child, each name. I hoped with all my heart that each child would feel seen and loved as I wrote his or her name on a piece of paper in big block letters. It reminded me of how meaningful handstamped jewelry was to each person in our community. A name reflected so much and captured such deep sentiment.

I began to help clean up from the snack time by gathering plates and cups. As I was wiping down one of the tables, a woman who worked in the kitchen made her way toward me. She looked to be about thirty years old, with short hair and a kind face. She seemed timid but determined.

"Will you write my name on a piece of paper?" she asked in Spanish.

I hadn't expected this. I paused for a moment as I processed her request.

"Of course!" I said with a smile as I pulled out the paper and pen from my bag.

It's not just the children. Each of us wants to be seen. Each of us wants to matter.

I felt humbled, a little teary-eyed, and a lot hopeful that this small gift would bless her. I prayed she would feel seen and loved—not just by me, but by the God of the universe. I wrote her name in big block letters, my hand shaking just a little bit, and handed it to her. She gave me a great big hug and said, "Gracias, gracias, gracias."

She was so thankful, but I had done so little—nothing really. But I knew it wasn't nothing to her. I also knew that God had done the work, not me. Just as David had simply been himself when he hugged the woman in church, I was just being me. I wasn't trying to be perfect; I was just showing up. God did the work.

My heart was full as our group climbed aboard the bus with the velvet curtains and made our way back to the hotel. Maybe my heart was a little softer, a little bit cracked, but so far, I had managed to protect my heart, to be strong, to not let poverty break me. Little did I know that God would soon crack my heart wide open.

Day four of our trip started off just as the other days had—eat breakfast at the hotel, grab a bottle of water, climb aboard the bus with the velvet curtains. We planned to make our way to a nearby village, participate in another Compassion program, and fall in love with a new group of amazing kiddos.

After we visited the Compassion program at the local church, we prepared to do a home visit. Then I saw the leaders gather in a huddle, making a quick change to our plans. They told us the family we had planned to visit was no longer available, so we were going to visit another family. This family lived at the top of a hill in a remote area where the roads weren't wide enough for the white bus. So our group shifted gears and prepared to hike a steep and winding path, past homes built from mismatched pieces of metal and wood, to make our way to the home of a little boy named Luis.

Luis lived with his brother, sister, and grandmother. We planned to chat with the grandmother and ask questions about how Compassion had changed their lives. I thought I knew what to expect, but at the top of the hill, as I walked out of the bright sunshine and into the tiny makeshift home with dirt floors, my heart nearly fell out of my chest. As my eyes adjusted to the light, I saw a little girl huddled in the corner of a couch. She was tiny— not only small but very thin. Looking at her, I knew at once she had a disability. This little girl was Luis's sister.

No. This is too much. My heart can't take it.

I thought about my David back home. I thought about the cupboard full of medicine and supplements we give him every day to keep him healthy, to ease his tummy pain, to help him breathe easier. I thought about the hospital down the street from our house that had helped us the numerous times when David had been very sick. David might well have died if we hadn't had that hospital nearby. I thought about the sturdy stroller we used to help David get around when he was too tired to walk. I thought about the drawers full of clothing that fit him just right.

Then I looked at the little girl. She wore a simple dress, clean and pressed. Her hair was pulled back into pigtail braids on either side of her head. Her arms were thin, and her legs were too weak to walk. I looked around their humble home. There was no medicine, no stroller, no dresser full of clothes, and no hospital nearby. There was hardly any food in their cupboard and no electricity.

Her grandmother made eye contact with me and told me in Spanish, "Her name is Jazmin."

I smiled back, and then I sat on the other side of the room, as far from Jazmin as I could sit. I didn't want to know her story;

I didn't want to hold her. I felt like my heart was about to break, and I wanted to keep my vow to stay strong.

This is too painful. I wish I'd never seen Jazmin.

We sat in a circle and began to chat with Jazmin's brother and grandmother. Their mom had left, unable to care for her children, so their grandmother had stepped in and was raising them.

I wanted to stay away from Jazmin, but I felt drawn to her like a magnet. A powerful force was pulling me toward her. It was like my soul was drawn to her soul. I tried to ignore it, to push it away. I even gripped the seat of my chair, but nothing worked. I stood up.

"May I hold her?" I asked her grandmother.

"Yes, yes," she said in Spanish, as she led me over to Jazmin and helped me scoop her into my arms and onto my lap.

Crap.

Tears began to fall, and my heart cracked open. I felt overwhelming love for this little girl. I had wanted to stay away to protect my heart, but I couldn't. I sat on the couch, holding Jazmin in my arms and falling in love with her.

Steve moved over and sat beside me.

"Our son has a disability too," he told Jazmin's grandmother.

Her eyes lit up. We were the same. We lived in different countries, spoke different languages, and had different skin tones and different socioeconomic situations, but we were the same. We were parents who loved our children. We each knew the pain of caring for a child whose life looks different because their body or mind doesn't work like it should.

We shared stories and details from our lives—David's favorite food, Jazmin's favorite snack, David's favorite toys, and Jazmin's favorite game. Steve and I connected deeply with both Jazmin and her grandmother. As we sat together, holding Jazmin and talking with her grandmother, we were on holy ground.

I thought about how our plans had changed at the last minute and how we ended up in this home. We hadn't planned to meet Jazmin, but God had other plans. Steve and I talked that evening about how profoundly impacted we were by Jazmin. We agreed it was a miracle that we ended up going to her home. I shared with him how I hadn't wanted to hold her but couldn't stay away. I was drawn to her; my arms had to hold her.

The next morning, we climbed on the bus with the velvet curtains once more and made our way to the local Compassion office for a tour. Each country has a main office with a staff that coordinates finances, projects, and details with local pastors. In turn, these pastors oversee the Compassion programs in their villages. We learned how pastors are trained and kept accountable to make sure the programs meet not only each child's needs but also the needs of that child's family.

After the tour, we walked outside into the garden to bask in a little sunshine. A woman named Katherine approached me. She was Dominican, but she spoke perfect English.

"I heard you met Jazmin and her grandmother yesterday," she said. "I met Jazmin a few months ago, and every day I have been praying that God would send someone to encourage her grandmother."

Her words stopped me in my tracks.

"Really?" I asked. I could feel a lump forming in my throat.

Meeting her wasn't an accident. We didn't just happen to go to Jazmin's house. God planned this whole thing.

God loved Jazmin, a little girl with a disability who lived at the top of a hill in a remote area in the Dominican Republic. To the world, Jazmin was no one, and yet to God, she was precious.

My short conversation with Katherine gave me more insight into the events of the previous day. I thought about how God had moved heaven and earth to answer her prayer. He took Steve and me on two plane rides, an hour-long drive on a bus with velvet curtains, and a long hike up a steep hill. He took us to a very specific place for a very specific purpose. I thought about how God so extravagantly demonstrated his love for Jazmin. He cared for her. In a world that says this little girl doesn't matter, God says, "She matters to me. She is worth every diamond, every pearl. She is beautiful and worthy. She is mine."

It was hard not to think about my own precious child. *What if David had been born at the top of a hill in a remote village in the Dominican Republic? What would David's life have looked like?*

God calmed my heart and told me, "I would meet David, just like I met Jazmin. I would meet David and provide for him, just like I do right now. It would look different; the landscape would be different; the circumstances would be different, but I am the same God. David is worth every diamond, every pearl. He is amazing. He is worthy. I love him, and he is mine."

I breathed in deeply, soaking up this beautiful thought.

Yes, I believe it.

I had seen it firsthand. God gave good gifts to his children. He loved Jazmin. He loved David.

I sat with this beautiful truth and let it soak into my heart.

Then God ambushed me with a whisper. *And you too. I love you, Lisa.*

I felt the lump in my throat. I wanted to push those words away. They were too tender, too precious. I didn't want to hear those words.

If I hear those words, if I let them in, I think my heart will fall to pieces.

"Yes," God whispered to my heart again, "just like I love Jazmin, just like I love David, just as they are worth every diamond and every pearl, you are too. I love you, Lisa. I love you just as you are. You don't have to do anything for me to love you. You don't have to be anything or say anything or look a certain way. Right here, right now, I love you."

I let the words in. I let them tear my heart into a million pieces.

I wept. *Why is this so painful? Why is this truth so hard for me to hear?*

The self-protective walls I had spent a lifetime building around my heart were starting to come down. Brick by brick, God was dismantling years of trying to be good enough, trying to prove I was worth loving. Now I finally understood. I never had to try. I never had to prove myself. I had always been loved.

I was not so different from Jazmin. What did she bring to God that he needed from her? She could not walk on her own. She could not feed herself. She could not read or write or speak. She had nothing to offer God—except her heart.

That was all he wanted.

With Jazmin's heart, God would do big, amazing things. He was using Jazmin's heart to change my heart. I came to God just as empty-handed as Jazmin did. All my life, I tried to be good enough, to be kind enough, to serve enough, so I could prove to God and others—and myself—that I was worth loving.

I couldn't fully understand it at the time, and maybe I never will fully understand it, but I was beginning to see—and to really believe—that I am loved just as I am. Beginning to see that it is God who does the work, not me.

I held this thought gently in my heart and considered it from all sides. *I am loved just as I am, not for anything I do or say or how I look.* It was a lovely thought, but it was also big and powerful. This thought could destroy my life as I knew it. This thought could change everything. I felt terrified.

I was beginning to understand I was not in control—and I had never been in control. I didn't want to believe that I came to God empty-handed. I wanted to believe I was strong and brave and important. I wanted to believe I was different from Jazmin. But now I saw that we were the same—needy and broken and beautifully loved just as we were.

I thought back to the woman who had asked me to draw her name in big block letters. I didn't have to try. I didn't have to do anything big or be someone important or look a certain way. I just showed up, and God did the work. God used me to give her a gift.

I felt peace wash over me. I could let go. I could stop trying. I could just be—and God would love me.

This truth was new and big—so big that it would take a long time to integrate it into my life, into the way I saw myself.

I was forever changed after meeting Jazmin. That day, I set out on a new path. I had seen new things; I had seen God's love in a new way. As I fell asleep that night, I prayed for Jazmin. "Lord, please keep her warm while she sleeps tonight. Please give her enough food to fill her belly, and most of all, Lord, I pray she knows how precious she is to you. I pray she knows she is seen and loved. Amen."

Then I added a P.S. "And me too, God. Help me to know how precious and seen and loved I am."

I wanted everything to be easy after that day. I wanted my new insight into God's love to bring nothing but sunshine and rainbows into my life. But things were going to get much messier before they got better. Things were going to get darker before the sun shone again. God was changing me. He was changing my heart, and change is often hard.

I didn't know it, but my world was about to be disrupted. My world was about to be rocked.

You Are a Poem

You are a poem,
A sonnet, a song,
Part of God's symphony—
You matter; you belong.

God crafted you well,
One word at a time.
He made you unique,
Verse by verse, line by line.

You are sewn together
With the words God said,
From the tips of your toes
To the top of your head.

You are a treasure,
A spoken work of art.
From elbows to knees,
He scripted each part.

With a whisper and a shout,
With rhyme and some prose,
God crafted your hair.
He created your nose.

The Artist inspired,
His pen moving fast,
He wrote out a ballad,

His design unsurpassed.

You were written with love,
Composing body and soul.
Each verse fits together.
You are complete; you are whole.

The quirky parts of you,
Harder to embrace,
Are how God draws you close
And shows you his grace.

The amazing part
Of the poem that is you
Is your beautiful heart
That shines bright and true.

God gave you a glow,
A light and a spark,
To show you the path
When things seem too dark.

Every step and misstep
Tells the story of how
God authored your course
And brought you to now.

Right here in this place,
Right now where you stand.
This is not a mistake.
He is holding your hand.

God wrote your journey,
Penned your innermost dreams.
He erased fear and shame;
He inked plans and schemes.

You are not forgotten;
You are not alone;
All is as it's meant to be—
You are loved; you are known.

Be quiet and listen;
Be still and you'll find
Your heart knows the way.
Your path will unwind.

You are a poem,
A sonnet, a song,
Part of God's symphony—
You matter; you belong.

chapter twenty-five

ALONE

I had glimpsed God's love for me a couple months earlier in the Dominican Republic. *Where is that love now?* I was trying to let go, trying not to control everything, trying to believe I was loved just as I was. But I didn't feel loved.

One evening after the kids were in bed, I walked upstairs—through the master bedroom and into the bathroom. I shut the door and locked it behind me, dissolving into tears as I sank to the floor. Overwhelmed and desperately sad, I cried until my body shook and my lungs gasped for air.

Then the sadness turned to anger. Rage coursed through my veins.

This is so unfair. I've worked so hard. I've tried so hard. I give so much, and it's never enough. Everyone always needs more from me. The house always needs tidying; the groceries always need buying; the laundry always needs folding; and the emails pile up in my in-box. My to-do list is never ending, but my energy supply is limited—and completely depleted. And not just my energy—I'm limited. I feel empty. My soul is empty. My heart aches.

The pain was unbearable.

I sat on the bathroom floor and grabbed a chunk of hair,

twisting it around my fingers and yanking as hard as I could. The physical pain felt like relief compared to my emotional pain, so I did it again. I looked at my hand, now full of hair, and cried harder. I lay on the bathroom floor and wept.

For so long, I had tried to push down these feelings of sadness, but I couldn't do it any longer. There was no more room for pushing things down. All the feelings were coming up, overflowing, exploding.

I'm alone. No one understands this pain. No one can comprehend how hard it is to do so much and fail constantly. I care for two children, one with special needs. I try to keep the house running and I work hard for our business—and I fail constantly. I am miserable. I hate my life. I hate myself.

I wished I could run away. I wished I could be alone forever—and just sleep. If I could crawl into a warm bed, I thought I could sleep for a week straight. I was so tired. So very tired. So empty.

At some point, I lifted myself off the bathroom floor and climbed into bed.

I tossed and turned all night. There was an emotional wall between Steve and me, built over months and years of misunderstanding, reinforced by hurt feelings and my fear of conflict. Turning toward him was too scary for me. I wanted peace between us. I didn't want to fight and scream and yell. I hated conflict. So I turned away.

I tried to push down my feelings of frustration and sadness, but they didn't go away. They only made the wall that separated us taller and stronger. Steve felt alone. I felt alone. We were next to each other, but so far away. We looked at each other, but we didn't see each other—all we could see were our own hurts and frustrations. There were times I despised him, and I was fairly certain he despised me as well. But I also loved him, and I desperately wanted him to love me too.

Earlier that day, he had leaned over toward me, kissed my cheek, and told me he loved me, but I didn't believe him. There were times I wanted to go over to him and wrap my arms around him and tell him how much I loved him—but I didn't. I turned away.

We'd been doing this painful dance for months. We would start to fight; he would get angry; and I would shut down. I hadn't left physically, but I had left mentally and emotionally. We talked about work, the kids, the house—but only on the surface. The important things, the things we needed to say most, went unsaid.

Now I was finally done. I was so tired of being overwhelmed. So tired of being angry. So tired of feeling like a failure. So tired of being tired.

I needed to be alone. I couldn't think straight anymore. I felt hollow, like I had lost myself completely. If there was a way for us to reconnect, I couldn't seem to find it. We had been in counseling for months, but nothing seemed to change. It was like the counseling had opened up pain inside each of us and only made things worse.

I want to be alone. I need to be alone.

I finally decided to tell Steve I needed time apart. I was frightened and desperate, and I couldn't see any other way.

I made an appointment with our counselor for later in the week, but time felt like it was standing still. Hours felt like days, and days felt like months.

How will Steve react when I tell him I want to separate?

How will our friends and family react?

How will our church react?

I felt I was turning my back not only on Steve, but also on our friends, our family, and our faith. I feared I would end up alone—but I already felt desperately alone. I was trying so hard,

and nothing was working. Things had to change. I had to change.
I could no longer live my life as I knew it.

We drove separately to our counselor's office and met up in
the parking lot. When I saw Steve, I wanted to run over and hug
him. I wanted to comfort him and tell him that everything would
be okay. But I didn't run to him; I didn't comfort him. I had tried
for so long to make everything okay, but nothing was okay.

I was about to tell Steve that I wanted to separate, so I tried
to reconnect with the anger and desperation deep inside me and
hold on to those feelings. I tried to remember why I wanted to
separate. *Perhaps if we take some time apart, I can find myself
again. If we don't see each other for a while, maybe we can start to
see each other again—not just with our eyes, but with our hearts.
Perhaps we can pause and then start over. Maybe next time we can
do things differently.*

We walked up the steps to our counselor's office, and I was
consumed by dread. It was a weight so heavy that I thought I
might crumble beneath it.

I loved him. I hated him. I wanted to be with him. I wanted
to run away. I wanted to scream. I wanted to cry. I wanted him to
hold me. I didn't want him to touch me.

I didn't know what I wanted.

I wished I could be anywhere but here.

Here I Am

Wherever I go, I am there.
Wherever I am, I find myself.
When I look in the mirror,
I see me looking back.

I look hard.

I look deeper.

Who do I want to be?

Strong and brave,

Trying new things,

Going new places,

Having adventures,

Kind and nurturing,

Gentle with others,

Gentle with myself,

Making time for quiet,

Time to be alone with myself,

Time to see myself.

I am beautiful and unique.

I am lovely simply because I am me.

There is no one else quite like me.

I am rare and exceptional,

Insightful and wise,

Loyal and honest,

Creative and confident,

Peaceful and calm.

chapter twenty-six

CLIFF JUMPING

We sat side by side on a love seat in the counselor's office. This wasn't our regular counselor—she had canceled our appointment because she was sick. But I couldn't wait any longer. I couldn't go one more day without sharing my heart—the deepest, darkest, scariest stuff. It was time. I had to tell Steve that I wanted to separate. I called another counselor we knew to see if he could schedule an emergency meeting with us.

We sat side by side, next to each other, but we did not touch. We knew each other so well, but we felt like strangers. *We're still a couple, but will we be a couple after this? We're together, but will we be together after I tell Steve what I have to say?* I felt like I was standing on the edge of a cliff, about to jump off. This was the hardest thing I had ever done.

"Lisa," the counselor said, "is there something you want to tell Steve?"

"Yes," I said, trying to keep my voice steady. I felt like my throat was closing, but I willed the words to come. I wanted to run out of the room. I wanted the ground to swallow me up. I wanted to call the whole thing off.

But I didn't run. The ground didn't swallow me up. I didn't

197

call the whole thing off. I jumped. I leaped off the cliff, terrified, not knowing what the future might hold. I left what was known behind me and hurdled into the unknown.

"Steve, I think we need to separate," I said.

The words were out there—in the real world. Time seemed to stand still. The words hung in the air. I simultaneously wished I could take them back and felt relieved I had actually said them out loud.

The look on Steve's face was a mix of confusion and desperation. My heart broke for him. I hated this, but I couldn't see any other way.

"What?" he asked.

"I think we need some time apart," I said again. "I need some time to think and figure things out."

The universe cracked into pieces. Our world fell apart. Steve was crying. I was crying. My head was spinning. I couldn't think or hear or see straight. It was like I had left my body. I felt numb.

The counselor was talking to Steve now. Everything was blurry, loud, confusing, and absolutely terrifying. It felt so dark in this new unknown place. I had jumped off the cliff, and I was falling fast. *Will I fall forever? Am I about to crash into the hard earth? What will the future hold?*

We sat on the love seat in the counselor's office for four hours. *What is happening? What does this mean? Who are we now? Who will pack a bag? Where will that person stay? How long will we be apart? Who will stay with the boys?*

After hours of back-and-forth negotiation, we decided that Steve would stay with a friend that night, but in the morning, I would drive a few hours south and stay with my sister for a few days. Steve would stay at home with the boys. Steve would hold down the fort—packing lunches, doing the school drop-offs, feeding the boys, carrying out the bedtime routines. I would go away and have some alone time.

I felt awful leaving the boys, but the idea of having some space and time with no responsibilities sounded like heaven. I needed a break. I needed time to regroup. I needed to stop falling through the air and find solid ground. I needed to stop taking care of everyone else and make time to care for myself.

We drove home separately. Life as I knew it was behind me now. Everything was different, unfamiliar, unknown.

We walked into the house together, our eyes red and our faces streaked with tears. Steve packed a bag to stay at a friend's house. I was so thankful that our friend had welcomed Steve to stay with him while we sorted through our mess.

I had ordered curry chicken and rice earlier in the day. The boys had eaten hours earlier, but leftovers were still out on the counter. Steve asked if he could have a plate of food before he left for the night.

"Of course," I said, feeling like it was the least I could do.

He ate and then packed an overnight bag, and we told the boys he would be back tomorrow. I walked him to the door, and we hugged for a long time.

How can I love him so much and still want to be away from him? How can I want to be both together and apart? I want him, but I want things to be different. I want him to be different. I want me to be different. I want us to be different. I want us to be together, but in a different way.

Steve drove away. I watched his car go down the street and turn the corner.

The world around me looked the same, but everything was different.

All was unknown. I felt disoriented, alone, scared to death.

I went into David's room first and tucked him into bed. I pulled his blankets up over his shoulders and tucked them around his sides, creating a warm, cozy space for him.

Lord Jesus, I prayed silently, *how will we explain this to David in words he can understand? How will we help him and comfort him as we go through this dark time? Help us, Lord. Give me wisdom. Give Steve wisdom. Keep your hand on David and comfort him in ways we cannot. Help us, Lord.*

I walked next door to Matthias's room to tuck him in.

"Hi, sweetheart," I said with a forced smile. I knew he knew. Matthias had a tender heart and was keenly aware of the tension in the house.

"Mom, is Dad coming back tonight?"

"He'll be back tomorrow," I said. "Then I'm going to go stay with Auntie Ellen for a few days. Dad and I love each other. We are working hard to learn how to love each other better."

I wondered if what I was saying made any sense at all. I could hardly make sense of the situation myself—how could I explain it to an eleven-year-old?

"Lord Jesus," I prayed out loud with Matthias, "please send your angels to watch over Matthias and keep him safe. I pray Matthias will know deep in his heart that he is loved. Amen."

Then I prayed silently. *Help us, Lord. Help me to love Matthias in the way he needs to be loved. Help Steve and me to make a safe space for him. Help us to process this mess with him in ways he can understand. Lord, if there is any way, please protect his young heart from the pain surrounding him.*

I said good night and walked out of Matthias's room, quietly closing the door behind me.

The boys were in bed. *After today, will their parents be together?*

Is this the day their lives change forever? Have I just blown their worlds apart? So many questions without answers.

I moved toward my bedroom with a heart so heavy that I thought it might fall out of my chest. My throat was tight. The tears were there, ready to come at any moment if I let them. It was an unbearable sadness.

So many questions.

Time. I need time. We need time.

I climbed under the covers, exhausted. This was the bed we had shared for seventeen years. *Will we ever sleep in this bed together again? Will we ever hold hands again? Are we us anymore? Who am I without him?* The thoughts were so scary that I pushed them away.

I fell into a dreamless sleep.

The next morning, I woke up and the memory of the night before washed over me like a dark wave. I moved through our morning routine on autopilot. Make coffee, bathe David, pack lunches, brush teeth. I grabbed an overnight bag and tossed in some clothes, my toothbrush, and my journal, and we all got into the car. I dropped the boys off at school and then headed down to Southern California to stay with my sister Ellen for a few days. Usually this kind of getaway would have me giddy with excitement, but today a dark fog surrounded me. A heavy sadness covered everything—and I was responsible. I was the one who had cracked the world in two. I was the one who broke Steve's heart. I was the one ruining everything. But I saw no other way. All I knew for certain was that I needed time to think—so I focused on that.

Take time. Breathe. Rest. Journal. Things will become clearer.

Stress and Worry

Stress and worry
Have helped me not.
My joy they've taken,
This moment forgot.

My thoughts bundled up
In fear of unknowns,
My mind distracted,
My present disowned.

Detached from what is,
I guess what may be.
I imagine the worst.
Dark and doom I see

Instead of the light
That always surrounds me.
I am safe and secure.
God loves me profoundly.

My path is before me.
God planned every part
Before my first step.
From the end to the start,

Life's mysteries to me
Are by God fully known.
I am his child.

He cares for his own.

When sorrow takes hold
And the light seems so dim,
His grace and love find me,
My hope is in him.

When the pain of this world
Crowds in to oppress,
My God gently holds me
And shows me his rest.

My worries don't help me,
I'm beginning to find.
They wreck and they ravage
The joy that is mine.

I am free; I can breathe.
Nothing can alter
The path I am walking.
My God will not falter.

Today I will practice
Letting go of control.
I am held by God's hand.
All is well with my soul.

I will learn to be still
And quiet the fear.
Today is a gift.
My God holds me near.

chapter twenty-seven

SPACE

The drive to my sister Ellen's house gave me four hours of quiet space. I thought; I cried; I listened to an audiobook; I prayed. I didn't have places to put these thoughts. I could not organize them or make sense of them yet—so they tumbled and swirled, into and out of my brain, around my head. And I let them. I reassured myself that, with time and space, my thoughts would become clearer; questions would be answered; things would make sense.

Please, Lord, I silently begged. *Please help things make sense.*

My sisters Chrissie, Susan, and Ellen had cleared their schedules for the evening so we could meet up for dinner. We headed over to a small Mexican restaurant and sat in a cozy booth. As the server brought chips and salsa, I felt safe and grounded with my sisters, yet also like I was falling through darkness and hurtling toward the unknown.

My sisters loved and supported me, no matter what. I was incredibly fortunate to have these three women beside me, and I felt the fullness of this blessing. I knew they would be there. I knew they would love me. I knew I could stay at their homes. I knew I could say anything, and they would listen without judgment.

I wondered if Steve was alone right now. I wished I could

comfort him, but I knew I could not. Instead of comforting him, I had done the opposite—I had hurt him. I wished I hadn't hurt him, but I couldn't see any other way. I prayed for friends to surround him. I prayed he felt loved and supported. I prayed he would find solid ground in the darkness.

Dinner with my sisters provided a moment of levity in a time of heaviness. We talked and shared our hearts. I cried a bit; we laughed a little. As we paid the bill, I suddenly felt exhausted. I wanted to be alone.

We hugged and said good-bye and headed our separate ways—Chrissie and Susan to their homes, Ellen and I the mile and a half to her home. As we walked up her porch steps, I told her I was going to head to bed. It was only eight o'clock, but I was spent. She understood. She had told me to take all the time I needed. She had no needs or agenda. She had welcomed me to her home so I could have space.

I pulled off my clothes and put on my coziest jammies. I climbed into bed, buried my head in the feather comforter, and cried. The tears came from deep inside, from a well that seemed like it would never run dry. I let myself cry and cry. I had nowhere to be; I had nothing to do; and I had no other demands on my time. I had space to cry, so I cried until I fell asleep.

I woke up the next morning as the sun peeked through the bedroom window.

I was at Ellen's house. I had no to-do list. No one needed or expected anything from me. The whole day was mine. I stretched out in the bed. No need to rush, I would take my time. I looked at the clock and realized that Steve was probably finishing the morning routine, packing lunches, and getting ready to head out the door to take the boys to school. I felt guilty. I should have been home helping with the morning routine.

I took a deep breath and let the guilt subside.

I needed space. As messy and crazy and dark and awful as it had been to get to this morning, I needed to be here. I needed to be alone with the sun peeking through the window and a day of nothingness stretching out ahead of me.

Space.

I breathed in as deeply as I could, held the breath for four seconds, and then breathed out slowly.

I could do whatever I wanted to do. I could take care of me. There was space for me today.

For another twenty minutes, I lay in bed, letting my thoughts tumble and swirl, into and out of my brain, around my head. I still could not make sense of them, but now the thoughts didn't seem quite as dark or scary. I got up, pulled on my walking shoes, and headed outside.

I walked up Ellen's street and through her neighborhood, up and down each street, like a boat following the course of a river winding back and forth. I had no time limit, no destination. I could walk as far as I wanted for as long as I wanted. I walked by each house and wondered who lived inside. *Are they married? Are they happy? Does the woman who lives there feel responsible for everyone else's needs and wants? Does she have a to-do list that overwhelms her? Does she have space in her life for herself?*

I tried to breathe deeply as I walked.

Space. Today I had space for me.

I suddenly felt overwhelmingly sad. I couldn't keep the tears from coming, so they began to roll down my cheeks. I blinked and turned around to head home. I stopped my zigzaggy wandering through the streets and walked a direct path back to Ellen's house. I had been walking for forty-five minutes, but it took only ten minutes to get home.

A shortcut.

I wished there could be a shortcut through this pain. I wished I had answers instead of questions. I wished I had confidence instead of fear. I wished things were neat and tidy instead of messy.

But there was no shortcut. There was no way to speed up this process. It had been a long and winding road that led me to this place—a place where I had become desperately sad and confused, a place where I felt completely lost. I knew I needed to walk a long and winding road to find my way back again. It would take time to find myself.

I had pushed myself away, set myself aside, and stuffed down my needs and wants for so long. I had told myself to become less so I could make others more—and in the process, I disappeared. It didn't work. It was never going to work. I was never going to be able to make others happy or control their thoughts and feelings. Control was an illusion—an attempt to earn their love. I believed if I could make them happy, they would love me, and look where it had led me—into a world where everything was upside down and crazy, dark and scary and unknown. My big plan didn't work—it was a disaster. I had nothing figured out.

The thoughts tumbled through my mind, swirling around. I could not make sense of them yet.

Doing Nothing

Doing nothing is not nothing.
Doing nothing is doing something important.
Doing nothing makes space for my brain to rest and my heart
    to heal.

Doing nothing makes room for breathing and thinking
     and being.
Doing nothing means not rushing.
Doing nothing takes discipline and practice.
Doing nothing used to make me feel guilty.
But I'm doing better at doing nothing.
Sometimes doing nothing means the most important thing
     gets done.

chapter twenty-eight

SADNESS

My shortcut took me quickly back to Ellen's house. Ellen was at work, and I had the house to myself. I pulled off my walking shoes and climbed back into bed. The sadness washed over me again. Tears came, and I didn't stop them.

I had space. Today, I could take time for whatever I needed and wanted. Right now, I needed to cry—and I cried for a long time.

The morning usually flew by—with breakfast, baths, and school drop-offs. I would often go to the grocery store and swing by the bank after I dropped off the boys. My days were filled with emails and meetings and tidying the house and coffee dates and decisions to be made. But today there was no to-do list. The only thing for me to do was to simply *be*. It was both luxurious and unsettling. I knew how to be productive, but I didn't know how to slow down, relax, and do nothing. I knew how to take care of other people, but I didn't know how to take care of myself.

The house was quiet. There was no music, no TV, no phone buzzing with texts. A few birds chirped outside and a ceiling fan hummed in the next room. I journaled for a while, jotting down random thoughts, hopes, and fears. I made myself a snack and then lay down on the bed with a book. After reading a few paragraphs, I put the book down. Doing nothing felt like all I could do. Doing nothing felt important. I knew deep down that I needed to do nothing. I needed this time. This was not wasted time. Questions flew in and out of my head.

Who am I if I'm not doing anything?

If I take time for myself, am I being selfish?

Am I bad mother?

If I'm not productive, am I worthwhile?

These questions were part of my journey, part of my healing, part of the reason I was where I was—desperately sad and tired and unhappy. These were important questions. I didn't push them away. I gave myself permission to make space for me, even though I knew that Steve was hurting and that it was hard on my boys.

I was hurting too.

I allowed myself to hurt—something I hadn't allowed myself to do in a long time. I had tried not to hurt so I wouldn't be a burden to anyone else. For as long as I could remember, I tried not to be sad so I wouldn't add stress to our family. I tried to be happy, upbeat, and easygoing. I had embraced Steve and the boys when they were hurting, but I hadn't allowed myself to hurt. I had pushed those feelings down.

The same thoughts I had on the night of the berry crumble disaster washed over me. I sat up and looked in the mirror. Just like my husband was a person, I was a whole person with all kinds of feelings, some enjoyable and some painful, but all of them necessary and real. Just like my boys were people who needed love and nurturing, I was a person who needed love and nurturing. There were four people in our family, and I was one of them. I counted. I mattered.

I had needs and wants, and they mattered because I was a person. Denying my feelings didn't make them go away. I could stuff them down for a while, but they were still there, under the surface, waiting to be felt. Being a person without needs and wants didn't make my needs and wants go away. Ignoring my needs and wants meant that little by little I was draining the joy from my life. I spent so much energy being needless and wantless that I had less energy for important things.

For so long, I believed that if I was a good wife and mom, if I could be good enough, I would be lovable. I tried to be two-dimensional so I wouldn't inconvenience others. I tried to give and not ask for much.

My chest felt hollow except for the ache—a nagging sadness I experienced as physical pain. I felt empty. It was like I had given away so much of myself that I was fading as a person. Disappearing. In the process of loving and wanting to be loved, I had lost myself and lost my way.

I wanted to love others, but I also wanted to love myself.

I wanted to meet others' needs, but I also wanted to acknowledge my own needs and take them seriously.

I wanted to listen as others shared their feelings, but I also wanted to feel my own feelings.

I wanted to stop trying to use beauty and material things to ease the sadness.

I wanted to stop trying to be good enough, happy enough, and easygoing enough—and open myself up to feel what I really felt. I wanted to be who I really was. Me, just me.

I wanted to feel the sadness. I wanted to stop pushing it down and let it bubble up and spill out. I wanted to feel every tear as it rolled down my cheek.

Yes, it hurts. It's painful. It's real. It matters. Let it be hard and ugly and imperfect. It deserves to be felt.

I pulled out my journal and started to list the things that made me sad. I tried not to think too hard or edit myself—I just wrote down whatever came to mind.

At the top of my list, I wrote down *David* and *Disability*. It sucked—it sucked for him. It wasn't fair that he had no words and couldn't speak. It sucked that he needed help with basic activities, such as eating and toileting. It sucked that he wasn't a typical teenager hanging out with his friends and playing video games. It sucked that he would never have a girlfriend, a first kiss, a wedding day, a newborn baby, a first job, a career. As I jotted down the list of things David would never experience, my chest heaved with sobs, and heavy tears flowed. It was so sad. So very sad.

It sucked for our family. It sucked that everything was more complicated because of David's needs. It sucked that we had to lug around a stroller or wheelchair and plan routes without stairs. It sucked that it was hard to eat in restaurants because halfway through a meal, David often got tummy pain and needed to get up and walk around. It sucked that David was often up half the night because his tummy hurt or he simply couldn't sleep.

It sucked for Matthias. He didn't have a typical sibling to share life with—to wrestle and argue and play with.

It sucked for Steve and me. Caring for David was exhausting. Knowing that his life would always look different was painful.

I cried for David. I cried for Matthias. I cried for Steve. I cried for me. I cried for every mom who has a child with a disability. I cried for how lonely it is to care for another human being day in and day out, and for how sad it is to know that for the rest of my life he will need the same care. I cried because the thought of losing David, of him dying and no longer needing care, felt worse—*so* much worse. Unimaginable. I cried because it was likely we would bury David. The thought of his casket, his funeral, the void he would leave behind, was unbearable. I cried because I loved David and I loved caring for him. I cried because I wanted him and I felt like I was betraying him by being honest about how hard it was to live with his disability. I cried because my feelings were messy and I couldn't make sense of them all.

The next item I wrote on my list of things that made me sad was *Marriage*. Marriage was *hard*. I had walked down the aisle with stars in my eyes and hope in my heart. I thought I had life and love figured out. We were going to do it right, do it better. We would work through conflict by having honest conversations and listening to each other. Now I wondered if we had made a huge mistake. Maybe we were never well matched. Maybe I chose the wrong person. Things were a mess—and we couldn't fix it. I cried for that young woman who had walked so confidently down the aisle. I cried for all the years I'd smiled and pretended not to be sad. I cried for every wife who feels unseen—not because her husband doesn't see her, but because she doesn't see herself.

Then I wrote down *Red Bowl* and let the words flow. My pen moved fast; the words were messy. I *did* want the red bowl. Even when I pretended not to want it, I really did want it. I tried not to care, but I did care. I cried for the little girl who decided one day to stop fighting for the red bowl. I cried for her willingness to settle for whatever she got, to settle for eating cereal out of an orange bowl or a yellow bowl because it was easier. I cried because she tried to be needless and wantless. I wished she had fought to keep needing and wanting. I wished she had known she was worth fighting for.

Finally, I wrote the word *Tired*. I was sad because I was tired of doing laundry; I was tired of cooking; I was tired of changing diapers; I was tired of email; I was tired of meetings; I was tired of the demands of being a wife and a mom and a business owner. I was so very tired.

I wrote it all down. Every single thing that made me sad. Then I let all the sadness come. I didn't push it down or pretend it wasn't there. I looked it in the eye—the brutal reality that life was hard; being human was hard; my life was hard.

I let myself grieve; I let myself feel the pain and the hurt; and I let myself cry.

Pain Is Not a Gift

Pain is not a gift from God.
It's what God does through the pain,
The way he molds us,
The way he enlarges our hearts to love more deeply
And opens our eyes to see more clearly—
This is the gift.

Pain is clarifying.
When we're grieving, everything else melts away.
Things that usually worry us seem trivial.
Pain shows us the truth. We are fragile creatures.
We come before God empty-handed.
In that humble, needy place, he meets us with love and grace.
We are changed in a way that can't be undone.
We are torn apart and lovingly sewn back together—each
        stitch piercing our tender hearts.
It's a deep, indescribable ache.
We will carry this ache with us always.
Slowly, the ache becomes part of who we are.
We would never wish for pain, but once on the other side,
        we wouldn't change it.

We've walked through fire, and we are not the same as we
    were before.
We've been through the darkest night and we've glimpsed
    hope.

As we heal, we see with new eyes.
As we heal, our hearts beat with new strength.
As we heal, we hold more joy.
Most amazingly, in his unknowable way, God uses the
    brokenness of pain to make us whole.

chapter twenty-nine

A LITTLE
BIT STRONGER

A text alert on my phone buzzed me awake. The sun was lower in the sky, but still bright. It was now afternoon. After all my tears, I must have dozed off. *No rush, no guilt. This is what I'm here for—to have space to grieve and cry and doze off midday if I need to.*

I moved my hand over the bed until I felt my phone and picked it up. It was a text from Steve.

> Hi, sweetheart. I am thinking about you. I hope you can take this time to rest. The boys and I love you so much. Let me know if you're up for talking on the phone this evening. I love you.

Such tender, encouraging words. I felt guilty—I should have been home with my husband and my boys instead of stealing time. I was taking what wasn't rightfully mine. Then I caught myself.

No. That is my old way of thinking. I do need time. I deserve time. It's okay to take care of me. I'm not stealing anything. I'm not bad. This is good. As hard as it is, this is right. I need time so I can love my husband better, love my boys better, and, maybe most importantly, know myself so I can love myself better.

Part of me missed Steve desperately. I wanted to talk with him. I wanted to call him right then and there and tell him, "I love you! Don't worry; I'm on my way home. Everything is going to be fine." But that too was part of my old way of thinking—of making promises I couldn't keep. I couldn't make everything okay. Everything was not okay. I knew I needed to let it be what it was—messy and imperfect.

Another part of me never wanted to talk to Steve again. I wanted to run farther away. I never wanted to go back to where we had been—the pain, the emptiness, the trying so hard to do the right thing and feeling like a failure.

Space. I didn't need to respond to Steve's text right away. I could make space to think and be. I pulled on my walking shoes again and headed outside. It was warmer now—the coolness of the morning was long gone. The sun shone through the trees with an almost magical glow. I took a deep breath and felt a gentle peace around me. There was nowhere else I needed to be. In that moment, everything was fine. I wished I could live in that moment forever.

On my morning walk, I had turned left from the walkway in front of Ellen's house. Now I decided to turn right. I would walk another winding path up and down the streets of Ellen's neighborhood, but in a different direction. I would walk by different homes and front yards. I would walk past homes filled with different families that had their own stories.

Something in me had shifted. I was wearing the same running pants and zip-up hoodie I had been wearing that morning, and my hair was still tied up in a curly, messy bun. But I felt different.

I felt sad, but not desperately sad. Something else had made its way inside my heart—it felt stronger and more stable. It felt like hope and maybe just a tiny bit of clarity.

My afternoon walk took me in the opposite direction. *Could I do the same thing in my life? Could I change the course of my journey? Could I say, "Hey family, hey friends, hey me, I know I've done things a certain way for a long time now, but I am going to start doing them differently. I am going to make more space in my life for me. I am going to say what I really think instead of what I think you want to hear. I am going to be kinder to myself. I am going to live with the belief that I am a whole person, a person worth loving—not because of what I do or what I say or how I look, but simply because I am a person. If you don't like the new me, that's okay, but I have to be me. I have to learn how to love myself. It's going to take a lot of bravery—I don't expect it to be an easy road for any of us. It will be messy and ugly and hard, but I have to do it. I want to do it. I will do it."*

I looked around and saw bright blue sky, vibrant green grass, and warm sunlight seeping through the trees. It was beautiful. I looked at my own heart, and it was messy—broken and hurting. I thought about Steve and saw the hurt I had caused him. I wished I could make it easier for him, but I couldn't. It had to get messy before it got better. I hoped he would be able to walk this rocky road with me. I wanted to be with him. I wanted to be married to him. But I couldn't be the same as I was before. I had to be stronger and braver and more honest. I had to lean in and fight instead of shutting down and putting up walls.

I had no idea what it all meant. I had no idea what it would look like for us, but I hoped we could create together a new marriage built on loving each other and ourselves.

That evening I texted Steve. Wanna talk?

A few seconds later, my phone rang.

"Hi, sweetie," I answered.

"Hey, baby," he said gently, his voice full of what sounded like both hope and fear. "How are you?"

"I'm okay. I've been walking a lot. Thinking a lot. Crying a lot. Sleeping a lot." I paused for a moment. "I miss you," I said.

He exhaled. "I miss you too, sweetheart. So much. I love you so much. I want you to come home. But, sweetie, more than that, I want you to take this time for you. Take time to rest. And when you're ready, we're here waiting for you."

His words were filled with love and generosity. He was for me. He wanted me to take time to heal. He wanted me to come home. Even though I had caused him so much pain, he still wanted to be married.

I felt his grace toward me, and it gave me hope. But I was not ready—not ready to get in the car and drive home. I was not quite strong enough yet. I needed more time to think and rest and cry and plan. I needed to get a little stronger before I could go back to real life.

Love Is Not Safe

Opening ourselves to love means
    taking down the walls around our hearts,
    and leaving our hearts vulnerable.
A vulnerable heart does not simply risk being hurt;
    it will be hurt.
Love is not safe.
I am imperfect.
You are imperfect.

We love each other imperfectly.

We hurt each other.

So why take the risk? Why love?

Because in the broken-down messiness of vulnerability,

    while we wade through the pain of sharp words

    and the loneliness of being misunderstood,

    we are met with the healing balm of forgiveness.

While we journey down an unexplored, windy path,

    sometimes hand in hand, sometimes with our backs to

        each other,

    we find something truly magical.

When we leave safety behind,

    we find truth,

    the truth that we are loved

    exactly as we are—broken and imperfect.

We leave safety behind to find something immeasurably better.

We find *love* abounding in grace and hope.

We find we were not safe before; we were simply numb.

Numbness is comforting.

Numbness means not feeling the deep, painful ache of our

    hearts

    being pulled and stretched and torn.

But numbness also means missing out on the exhilarating joy

    of being known—

    the joy of being seen just as we are,

    the joy of being accepted,

    the joy of being called worthy,

    the joy of hearing the God of the universe say, "You are

        enough."

In that place of power, we look shame directly in the eye

    and say, "You are a liar."

Now we know the truth.

We leave safety to find freedom abounds.

We are free from the fear that held us prisoner.

The sun shines on us,

    warming our shoulders,

    filling our hearts with peace.

We soak it up,

    knowing we are loved

    just as we are.

chapter thirty

HALFWAY

I spent a couple more days at my sister's house and then decided I needed to be even more alone, separate, apart from those I knew and loved, those who cared about me. I craved being totally alone.

The day before I left Ellen's house, I went to Target to pick up some food and browse the aisles. I loved Target, and I sometimes joked that it was my second home. I parked my car far from the front doors—I wasn't in any hurry, and I didn't mind walking. Over the last few days, I had tried to soak up fresh air and sunshine, rest, write, and just be with myself without any pressure. The walk from my car to the entrance of Target felt like another way to slow down and rest.

As the automatic sliding glass doors parted and I made my way inside, I immediately smelled popcorn and saw people grabbing shopping carts and walking the aisles. I heard the shuffling of carts and a baby crying. There were bright lights and bold colors. All of my senses suddenly felt overwhelmed. My heart was beating fast in my chest, and I couldn't catch my breath. I grabbed a cart and headed toward the women's clothing section. I scanned the first aisle to see if it was clear, but there was a woman looking at cardigan sweaters. The next aisle was open—no people, no carts—so I turned down it and moved closer to the wall. I found a safe spot between two sale racks and took a deep breath.

It's okay. Breathe.

I took another breath, held it for a count of four, and then exhaled while counting to four, just as my therapist had encouraged me to do in moments of fear or tension. Then I did it again.

It's okay. It's okay. It's okay.

I could feel my heart slowing, but I knew my best course of action would be to grab the food I needed and head back to my sister's house.

I concentrated on my list and the task at hand. I avoided eye contact with strangers as I made my way to the checkout lane. My head was fuzzy as I forced a smile for the clerk and swiped my card. I was trying to act normal, but I felt overstimulated and overwhelmed. I made my way back to my car, climbed inside, and closed the door.

Relief. *I'm alone. It's okay.*

I sat for a few minutes trying to regroup.

Am I going crazy? I hadn't expected to feel overwhelmed by Target. I thought a Target run would be relaxing, but it was anything but relaxing.

Space. *I need space. It's okay to need space.*

That evening, I booked a room at a little hotel in Santa Barbara for a few nights. Santa Barbara is a beach town located halfway between Southern California and San Luis Obispo, where we lived. A few nights alone in a hotel sounded wonderful—plus I would be near the ocean, which is calming and healing.

I thanked Ellen profusely for her generosity. She loved me and opened her arms to me while I was so low. The use of her spare bedroom was a gift and a respite for my hurting heart.

Then I tossed my overnight bag into the back seat and drove the two hours north to Santa Barbara—and two hours closer to home.

Closer. It was a step in the right direction. I wasn't ready to go home yet, but I was ready to go halfway. Maybe in a couple more days my heart would be ready to go home.

I checked into the hotel, walked to my room, and stepped inside. As the door swung closed behind me, I exhaled.

All mine. This space is all mine for the next couple of days.

Those few days in the hotel were filled with resting, reading, walking near the ocean, and journaling. I slept a lot. It wasn't just my body that needed rest; my soul needed it as well. I read books that encouraged me, especially *Rising Strong* by Brené Brown and *Self-Compassion* by Kristen Neff. These books were water to my thirsty, tired soul. They gave me words for the ache in my heart and clarity for the confusion in my mind.

I listened to audiobooks as I walked near the ocean. With every step, life-giving truths cemented themselves in my heart. With every step, I gave my heart space to speak to me. With every step, I got to know myself a little better. With every step, I gained strength and insight into the person I was made to be. With every step, I walked away from my old life and toward the unknown. With every step, I breathed out lies I had told myself for so long and breathed in true and beautiful thoughts.

Back in the hotel room, I picked up my journal to write down thoughts that had come to me while I was walking. My journaling started as random words, disconnected thoughts, and sometimes even sketches. But after a couple days, my thoughts were beginning to take shape. One thing was clear—I wanted to make more space in my life for me. And my need for more space wasn't going to be met by scheduling a pedicure every other week—I needed much more than that. I needed to take pressure off myself so I had time to heal and grow.

It had been a long time since I had given up fighting for the red bowl—given up asking for the things I wanted and needed—and it was clear to me now that my giving-up strategy hadn't worked. It was time not only to ask for what I wanted and needed, but to fight for it. It would be disruptive to our family, but I knew there was no way around it. I needed space to be me. I needed space to heal and grow. I could no longer live needless and wantless. It was time for me to be a whole person. I was beginning to see there was space for me to be me—that my family *needed* me to be me.

I decided to make a list of things I needed to change once I returned home. I tried to think big, to identify what I really wanted and needed, not just what I thought I was allowed to ask for. How could my family meet my needs and wants if I never made my needs and wants known? It was time to speak truth and make changes.

My list began to take shape.

Cancel gym membership. After my Target run a few days earlier, it was clear to me that I needed more alone time. Instead of going to the gym, I would continue walking and hiking. That would enable me to move and breathe and also give me times of solitude.

Do less cooking. Cooking was time-consuming and stressful. I no longer had the energy for it, and I needed a break. I would remove the stress of cooking from my daily activities. Instead we would fix simple meals or order food to be delivered to our home.

Spend less time in the office. I felt depleted by meetings, emails, and administrative tasks. I could delegate some of my responsibilities for the business. We had a capable team that could fill in the gaps.

Find a regular babysitter. I needed help with David. We had nurturing sitters who were happy to meet David's needs and whom he adored. I could share the load of caring for David with others.

Make time for naps. I needed to sleep. I wanted to sleep. My mind and body and soul needed rest.

Make time to be with my sisters. I needed routine and scheduled times to process with them and fill my soul. I would make time with my sisters a priority.

Schedule regular dates with Steve. We needed more fun in our marriage. We also needed time to be together, just the two of us, to let our hearts connect. We could go out to eat, talk, laugh, and see a movie—just the two of us.

Speak my truth. Sharing my honest thoughts and feelings was going to be the hardest change of all. I was so used to pleasing people that the thought of displeasing people—of not saying or doing what they wanted me to—was terrifying. *What if they don't love me anymore?* The fear was real, but deep down I knew that unless people saw the real me, unless they knew my honest thoughts and feelings, they couldn't love the real me anyway. I had to let them see the real me.

I sat back and looked over my list. It was bold. It was honest. It was exciting. It was terrifying. It was necessary. The list felt tangible. It gave me a glimpse of what might be and helped me envision a life where I could thrive.

My heart was getting ready. I was halfway there.

Love Is . . .

Love is . . .
Holding hands,
Listening to my heart,
Listening to your heart,
Saying "I'm sorry,"
Forgiveness,
Beginning again,
Bed head mornings,
Kisses good night,
Easy and natural,
Harder than I ever expected,
Empowering,
Humbling,
Worth it.

chapter thirty-one

COMING HOME

I had been away for more than a week. I'd been away from my family, but very much *with myself*—more with myself than I had been in a long time. It was hard to believe I had taken so much time away for myself, but I knew it was necessary. I needed space, and as hard as it was for me to ask for it, my family had accommodated me. Because Steve willingly took care of the boys, the house, and the business, I had time to rest, cry, journal, walk, read, and learn to be present with myself—time to be quiet and think and simply *be*.

Now it was time to go home. I missed Steve; I missed the boys; I missed the house. As hard as it had been in recent times, I missed our life together. I wanted to go back to real life and start making changes. I packed up my small bag with the few things I had brought with me—my workout pants, hoodie, running shoes, favorite jeans, and the journal that had been beside me during my time away. I turned in my room key and headed toward the car.

As I put my bag into the trunk, I noticed that my chest felt tight. Being away was a respite. I had soaked up the downtime, relishing every minute I'd had to heal and rest, to grow and get stronger. The last ten days had been good for my soul. I felt clearheaded and stronger. I no longer felt desperately sad and empty. I felt hopeful, but I also felt something else. *Why is my chest so tight?* I sat with the feeling for a moment, trying to name it.

Fear. That's what it was.

Going home felt scary. I didn't want things to return to the way they had been. I didn't want to fall into my old pattern of setting aside my needs and wants to please others. I wanted to make space in my life for me. I knew that Steve and the boys would understand—they had literally just given me ten days of space—*but what about me?*

Am I strong enough to change? Am I brave enough to ask for what I need and want? Am I willing to let things be messy and engage in conflict if necessary?

I took a deep breath and climbed into my car. It was only a two-hour drive, but I wasn't expected home for a few hours. I could take my time—no rush.

I can do this. I can do this. I can do this. I pulled out of the hotel parking lot and headed toward the freeway. I connected my phone to the car and put on some mellow music, but I turned it off after a couple minutes. It was overstimulating. I needed quiet right then.

Will he love me? It was one of a host of questions I asked myself over and over as I drove through Santa Barbara toward home. *Am I pretty enough? Am I good enough? Am I worthy of Steve's love?*

The questions rolled through my mind, one after another, on repeat, as the fear in my chest intensified. It was as if every mile closer to home was a mile farther away from me. I was afraid of losing myself and losing hold of the clarity I had found over the last ten days.

I pulled off the freeway and into a gas station. Even though my tank was half full, I pulled up to a pump. I needed a moment to regroup. I looked around, relieved there was no one else in sight.

I turned off the car and sat back in the driver's seat. I took a deep breath, counted to four, and then exhaled for a count of four. I sat for a moment and then did it again.

I went to the trunk of my car and pulled out my journal. I wanted to write down something that would help me hold on to what I had learned over the last ten days. To my surprise, a little poem came out. Line by line, I wrote down my thoughts in rhyme.

> *I am me, just me,*
> *A one-of-a-kind, my own unique me.*
> *When I'm not fully me, when I wear a disguise,*
> *I get lost in the fog, I feel empty inside.*
> *Every day I am changing and growing to be*
> *The me that is braver, the me that is free.*

It was just a few lines, but these words reflected my heart. All I had to be was me. Just me—nothing else. *Deep breath.* I read the first line over again.

I am me, just me.

I didn't have to be good enough. I didn't have to be perfect. I was already loved. God made me *me.* I was okay if I made mistakes. I could own my mistakes and ask for forgiveness. I could forgive myself. God wanted me to be me. I didn't have to have this all figured out. I could be me, with all of my messiness and confusion, learning as I went. I whispered these gentle truths to myself and felt a calmness wash over me.

I topped off my half-full tank, pulled out of the gas station, and got back on the freeway.

Over and over as fear gripped my chest and questions ran through my head, I reminded myself of the simple words I'd written at the gas station.

I am me, just me.

The drive went quickly. I pulled into our driveway and paused for a moment, both relieved and terrified to be home. I slowly got out and retrieved my bag from the trunk. I opened the front door, and Steve greeted me with a bear hug and a kiss. As he held me in his arms, I was surprised to realize that it felt completely normal. It was us—just Steve and me. We were still us. On the kitchen counter was a gorgeous bouquet of flowers.

"I am so glad you're home, sweetheart," Steve whispered in my ear. "Let's just take our time and be gentle with each other, okay?"

"Okay, sweetie," I said as I leaned into his chest and let him hold me tight.

"I love you, Lisa," he said as he kissed the top of my head.

"I love you too, Stephen," I said.

I was home.

If You Could Read My Heart

If you could read my heart,
You would find the words
Hope,
Peace,
Joy,
Written over and over.
I am surrounded by blessings,
But also
Fear,
Shame,
Worry.
Am I enough?

If you could read my heart,
You would find the words
Brave,
Honest,
Present,
Written over and over.
My days are full of connection,
But also
Scared,
Quiet,
Hiding.
Do I matter?

If you could read my heart,
You would find the words
Creative,
Imaginative,
Unique,
Written over and over.
My mind is full of ideas,
But also
Hesitation,
Uncertainty,
Wondering.
Am I silly?

If you could read my heart,
You would find the words
That write my story
One letter at a time.
You would see scribbles

And eraser marks

And do-overs.

But the most important words

Are written over and over

In BIG bold letters

On every page of my heart

As a reminder of what is true:

I AM LOVED no matter what.

chapter thirty-two

A NEW BEGINNING

Coming home wasn't the end of my journey, but it was a new beginning—a messy one.

Those first two days, Steve and I were especially gentle with each other. Our relationship felt fragile, like our marriage was a cracked glass that could shatter at any moment.

What now? How do we do this? Who am I?

We had been in counseling for more than a year when I told Steve I needed a break. There were times when it seemed that bringing our feelings and hurts to the surface only made things worse. When I told Steve I wanted to separate, I felt like our marriage counseling had been a waste and a failure, but now I was beginning to see that it was necessary for our marriage to fall apart. Things had to get messier before they could get better. We had to walk through the darkness to find the light.

Our therapist encouraged us to individually attend a week-long workshop at a retreat center in Arizona called The Meadows. The workshop aimed to help people identify false beliefs and gain clarity in their personal lives so they could improve their relationships. I would be part of a small group made up of other people who wanted to heal and grow. I agreed to go, hoping that if I committed to doing the work, Steve would agree to do his work. Deep in my heart, I believed he was the one who needed to change. He needed to love me better, see me more, and be kinder to me. I thought I had my stuff pretty much figured out.

I was wrong. My time at the workshop completely changed my perspective.

When I arrived at the retreat center, I was filled with fear. I knew I would have to face my pain head-on. I walked into our meeting room on Monday morning with shaky knees. I felt vulnerable and exhausted from our marriage crisis. I hoped I could learn the skills I needed to be in a healthy marriage with Steve. If I could understand him better, maybe our marriage would be better.

Over the course of the week, I opened myself up, broke down, and began to put the pieces back together again. For the first time, I saw my part in the disintegration of our marriage. I had tried to please Steve to the point of losing myself. He wanted a wife who was strong, opinionated, and honest. For so long, I had felt powerless, pushing aside my needs and wants. I wasn't being me. I was trying to be the wife and mom I thought Steve wanted me to be. I was trying so hard, but all that trying was making things worse, not better.

Our disconnection wasn't all Steve's fault; I surely had played a part too. I was trying to manage and control everything to make our marriage work. I was trying to be good enough, to be lovable, to avoid conflict, to avoid the messiness. But how could he see me if I didn't show him myself? How could he love me if he didn't really know me? How could we be close if I continued to put up walls?

A couple weeks before, while I was staying at my sister's house, I had begun to see that I couldn't change Steve. I still wanted him to change, but I knew I wasn't the person to do it. Now I real-ized I needed to change myself. I needed to stop worrying about Steve and start working on me. I needed to take the energy I was wasting on trying to change him and put it toward making my own positive change—changing my false beliefs and the lies I had lived with for so long.

The blinders came off, and I saw my own unhealthy patterns for what they were. The false beliefs that had driven me for so long were not only hurting me; they were hurting *us*. Steve had his own work to do, and he was doing it, bravely engaging in his own healing process. I needed to do my work too. I needed to heal and grow.

After returning from the retreat center, I went to work on making changes. I made space for myself by clearing my schedule, canceling my gym membership, and cooking less. Steve also made space for me. He took on more responsibilities for the business, which gave me more time to rest and heal. He agreed to simple dinners and having food delivered. We slowed down.

We talked more and had the honest, difficult conversations I'd previously worked hard to avoid. Sometimes these conversa-tions escalated into arguments. A few times, when our feelings were hurt and our defenses were high, we screamed and I threat-ened to leave again. In those heated moments, I was convinced that our marriage was beyond saving. It felt too hard—and it *was* hard. It was excruciatingly painful. Change is hard. I wasn't sure our marriage could be salvaged, but I wanted to try. We were both willing to try.

It's now been more than two years since we first started to make changes. It's still not easy, but it's so much better. We engage in conflict more, but we also snuggle more. We've learned how to listen to each other. We've learned to own what's ours and not blame each other. It's still messy. We still drive each other crazy, but we also have more fun together.

I am learning to speak my truth—to say what I think, even if it might hurt Steve. I know now that not being honest will hurt him more in the long run. Every time I speak my truth, I grow stronger, more present, less afraid. When I speak my truth, I see myself and let others see me for who I really am.

I am learning to stop trying to please other people. When I feel the urge to patch things up prematurely, to avoid conflict, to gloss over whatever is not okay, I resist. I wait. I sit still in the mess and remind myself that I am lovable.

I am learning to accept help in caring for David. It takes a lot of time and energy to care for David's special needs. He needs help eating, bathing, and dressing. He takes medication four times a day. He has a list of specialists he needs to see regularly. For so long, I tried to shoulder the burden of his care by myself. But I need help. I can love David and be a good mom even if I'm not the one providing all his care. We have a regular sitter who comes in almost every day. It has been life-changing support—not just for me, but for all of us.

I am learning to make space for quiet and solitude. I take time to be alone and listen as God speaks to my heart. I put on my walking shoes and go for long, solitary walks. I nap a couple times a week. Sometimes I set the timer for ten or twenty minutes, and I simply sit quietly on the couch. Those quiet moments bring me peace and clarity.

I am learning to feel my feelings, especially the ones I don't want to look at, such as sadness and anger. I call my feelings by name, and then I sit with them in all the pain and discomfort. I no longer push them down or cover them up. I let myself cry and scream.

I am learning it is okay to make mistakes. When Steve and I have conflict, I own my part and apologize when I hurt him or wrong him. I can make mistakes and still be lovable. Even if everything falls apart and Steve stops loving me, I am lovable. The God of the universe loves me. It is all okay. I have hope. Even in the darkest places, I believe that God will meet me there with grace and love. I believe it, because every time I've been in a dark, lonely place, God has met me there.

I am learning to let go of trying to control everyone and everything around me. I cannot change my husband or my children. I cannot change my friends or my family. I can only change me.

I am learning to bravely love my husband, my children, my family, my friends, and, perhaps most importantly, myself.

Love Is Grand

You and me,
Me and you,
Side by side,
We are two.

Downs and ups,
Ups and downs,
Sometimes smiles,
Sometimes frowns.

Weak and strong,
Strong and weak,
Hold me close,
Kiss my cheek.

Tears and joy,
Joy and tears,
Speak your truth,
Face your fears.

Pain and hope,
Hope and pain,
Always changing,
Not the same.

Near and far,
Far and near,
Always precious,
Always dear.

We and us,
Us and we,
We are one,
Family.

Hand and heart,
Heart and hand,
Life is messy,
Love is grand.

chapter thirty-three

A HEARTFELT FRIEND, A HEARTFELT GIFT

My phone buzzed with a text alert. Hey friend, I know you're busy, but can you swing by today? I have a Christmas gift for you.

I was a couple blocks away from Susie's house when I read her text. Christmas was our busy season with the business—as in, *crazy* busy. Steve and I ran from one thing to the next, often in opposite directions. There were last-minute marketing decisions, newsletters to approve, manufacturing numbers to watch, and customer service emails and calls to return. Our team worked incredibly hard over the few weeks of the Christmas season. Steve oversaw it all, making sure things ran smoothly, and I jumped in when needed, dividing my time between the boys, the business, and preparing for our own family Christmas celebration.

Susie's text came at a particularly busy moment. I was headed to the office for a quick meeting and then needed to swing by the grocery store for eggs and apple juice. It seemed like every day I needed to run to the store for something. If I'd been more organized, I could have combined trips to the grocery store and been more efficient, but with the rush of the season, I didn't feel like I had time to get organized. My days were filled with running from one errand to the next, throwing in a load of laundry, returning emails, sitting in meetings, and grabbing a few necessary items from the grocery store. On this particular day, picking up eggs and apple juice was a priority so we could have our usual family breakfast the next morning. Even in the busyness, family breakfast was an unchanged part of our routine.

I was tempted to wait to respond to Susie's text. I knew she wouldn't mind. She knew how crazy our lives were, but I also wanted to see her. She was one of my dearest friends—a woman who knew my heart, my passions, and my imperfections, and yet who loved me just as I was. She was honest and insightful, often able to put into words what I was feeling better than I could. She was intuitive and committed to growing and learning so she could be a whole person, while encouraging others to do the same. She was amazing, and I loved her.

I only have a couple minutes, I texted, but I can swing by right now.

Perfect! she texted back. A moment later, I walked up her steps, past her garden pots overflowing with succulents, and knocked on her green front door.

"Come in!" she called from inside.

I opened the door and stepped inside, greeted by her colorful decor and the delicious aroma of a burning cinnamon-scented candle. She smiled as she came out of the kitchen carrying her sweet baby girl, Bella. She wrapped her arms around me in a big hug, and we squeezed each other tightly. I immediately wished I could cancel everything on my to-do list and spend the afternoon sitting on her cozy sectional sipping coffee and sharing our hearts, but I only had a few minutes. I soaked up her smile and her hug.

In the busyness of the Christmas season, I hadn't known how much I needed to see my good friend.

"I have a gift for you," she said. "It's just a little something, but I think you're going to like it." We sat down, and she handed me my gift, beautifully wrapped in a polka-dot bag with red tissue paper.

"Open the gift first," she said. "Then read the card."

I dug through the red tissue paper and pulled my gift out of the bag. I carefully unwrapped it and caught my breath. There in my hands was *a red porcelain bowl*. It was deep red, like ripe cherries, and had raised dots around the top edge. The bowl was shiny—pretty enough to keep on the counter. It was the perfect size for a large bowl of cereal—one of my favorite comfort foods. I held the lovely bowl in my hands and smiled at her.

"Now read the card," she said. I reached for the white envelope, slid my finger under the sealed flap, and pulled out the card. I could feel my throat tightening a bit and my heart beating faster. I took a deep breath and began to read.

Dear Lisa,

    A couple months ago, you told me the story of when you were a young girl growing up with so many siblings. You recalled how every Saturday morning, it was a race to see who could get to the kitchen first to secure the coveted red bowl. You also shared how one day you stopped fighting for the red bowl. You decided it was easier to let others have what they wanted. You decided it was easier to settle for second best.

    Thank you for sharing that story with me. It touched my heart and helped me to understand you in a new and deeper way. After you shared your story, I knew exactly what I was going to get you for Christmas.

It has been a joy to find a kindred friend like you. I bought this red bowl as a reminder that you are worth it. You are deeply loved, valuable, and cherished. You are worthy of the red bowl. I pray it will be a reminder of God's deep joy and delight over you. Like we say to Bella every night at prayer time, "You are seen. You are safe. You are loved."

Bless you, friend. I pray that you continue to offer your beautiful, open heart to the world—and I pray that you ask for the red bowl.

I love you.

Susie

The words blurred together as tears began to roll down my cheeks. Susie was reminding me that I deserved good and beautiful things. She gave me this red bowl as a symbol that I could have needs and wants. There was enough space for me to be me. I took another deep breath and looked at the red bowl sitting on my lap, and then I looked again at Susie. There were tears in her eyes too, and the sweetest smile on her face.

"Wow, friend," I said quietly. "This is an amazing gift." I was having difficulty putting my thoughts into words. I was so moved, so incredibly touched, but also afraid that if I tried to speak, I would sob uncontrollably. I felt seen and known. I felt encouraged and emboldened. I felt hopeful. I held Susie's gift in my hands and let the tears flow. She wrapped her arms around me and hugged me tightly. We sat together for a few moments as I soaked up the beauty of Susie's gift. Her gift spoke directly to my heart—encouraging me and giving me fresh insight.

Then I had to leave Susie's home all too soon. I climbed in my car, running a few minutes late for my meeting. The afternoon flew by as I ran errands, picked up eggs and apple juice, quickly cleaned the kitchen, and ordered a last-minute pizza for dinner.

That evening as we settled down and got ready for bed, I read Susie's card again. I let the tears flow once more. I let myself feel loved and seen by my precious friend. I soaked up the truth in her card. *I am worthy of the red bowl.* Then I happily poured myself a large bowl of Lucky Charms and treated myself to a bedtime snack in my very own shiny red bowl.

I knew it would take time, practice, and bravery, but this life-changing truth was taking root in my heart: *I can have needs and wants. I am worthy of love.* This red bowl would become a regular reminder that there was space for me to be me. I was worth fighting for. I was worthy of the red bowl.

I Am a Metaphor

I am the sun
With bright warm rays
Shining my light on others—
Shining.

I am a heart
With an easy, steady, ongoing beat
Giving life—
Giving.

I am a house
With sturdy walls, a haven for rest

Holding a safe place—
Holding.

I am a blanket
With thick yarn knitted in rows
Covering to comfort and soothe—
Covering.

I am a tree
With long, strong branches
Reaching toward the sky—
Reaching.

I am a book
With new words and big ideas
Sharing my adventures and stories—
Sharing.

I am the clouds
With white billows as far as the eye can see
Floating gently along—
Floating.

I am the morning
With openness and new opportunities
Beginning again, afresh—
Beginning.

I am the wind
With stunning force and power
Moving through and over and beyond—

Moving.

I am a bird
With wings to fly far and wide
Gathering bits and pieces for a nest—
Gathering.

I am a love letter
With handwritten notes of affection
Reminding the reader of abundant love—
Reminding.

I am me
With all of my laughter and pain and beauty
Being me in all my complexity—
Being.

chapter thirty-four

BRAVE LOVE

S tep by step, I am learning to love bravely.

I am learning that loving Steve is a messy, imperfect, brave love. It requires time and forgiveness, a willingness to break down walls and be openhearted. Bravely loving Steve means being willing to engage in conflict, to speak truth, to stay when I want to run.

I am learning to love both my children—to let them be exactly who they are without trying to make them conform to who I expected them to be. To bravely love them by letting them feel what they feel, by letting them make mistakes.

I am learning to bravely love David, not by overlooking his disability, but by accepting it for what it is—hard and painful, but also part of *him*, part of the sweet boy I love so much. He is amazing and beautiful and soulful and makes our lives so much better. He has changed the world in unexpected ways. He is not a mistake. With brave love, I see that he is a truly incredible human being, and I accept him just as he is.

I am learning to love Matthias in all his quirky insightfulness. He has always had his own thoughts and opinions. He has always loved art and had a vivid imagination. I want to love him with open hands, refusing to pin all my hopes on him as my "typical" child. I am learning that Matthias is just who he is meant to be—and I love him just as he is.

I am learning to bravely love my parents, my siblings, my friends, my coworkers—seeing each person as an individual, accepting them for who they are, with all their strengths and weaknesses. They each have their own spark.

And I am learning what may be the bravest love of all—to love myself just as I am. Brave love requires looking in the mirror and, even more, into my own soul and embracing what I see. It means acknowledging all my gifts and strengths, as well as all my failures and mistakes, and accepting myself just as I am. With brave love, I can rest in the knowledge that the God of the universe loves me just as I am. I don't have to change anything, prove anything, be anything—except me. Brave love doesn't always come easily or quickly, but it is simple and powerful.

When I love bravely, I am free.

Free to stop worrying about what others think of me.

Free to stop proving I am enough.

Free to fight instead of going with the flow.

Free to succeed.

Free to fail.

Free to feel all my feelings—happy, sad, silly, angry, desperate, tired, peaceful.

Free to be me—nothing more, nothing less.

The God of the universe created me and loves me.

Me.

Just as I am.

If I truly believe this, it only makes sense to love myself too.

To believe I am enough.

To believe I am loved, no matter what I do.

I can love myself.

I will love myself.

It will take time and practice, but I commit myself to the process of brave love.

I commit to looking at myself in the mirror and saying, "I love you."

I commit to celebrating and enjoying the endless beauty around me, knowing I can never own or possess it. It is a gift from God for me to receive and share.

I commit to seeing the beauty in myself—not just the surface beauty of my face or my body, but a beauty much deeper and more powerful. The beauty of a spark placed inside me by the God of the universe. A one-of-a-kind, uniquely amazing light that is all mine. It's beautiful. It makes me *me*. I love that God gave me my own spark. I love my spark! I love me.

I commit to letting my light shine—to being me, to saying what I think, to creating and living and loving out of this spark within me.

I commit to believing that, just as I have my own spark, each person has his or her own spark, a truly beautiful light that comes from within. Loving myself provides a solid and necessary foundation for loving others—my family, my friends, my coworkers, and even strangers.

I commit to brave love.

MY BRAVE LOVE MANIFESTO

1. I will make space for quiet. I'll find a cozy place where I can be alone with myself, a peaceful spot where I can listen to my heart. I'll listen closely and without judgment, believing the God of the universe has placed deep wisdom there.

2. I will remind myself that the God of the universe made me *me*. The God of the universe loves me. I don't have to please others, try harder, or be better. I am loved just as I am.

3. I will look in the mirror, look myself directly in the eye, and say, 'I love you.' I'll keep doing this, even if it's awkward, until it sinks in and I believe it.

4. I will happily share a piece of cake with you. Sometimes I'll give you the bigger half, but sometimes I'll take the bigger half for myself, believing we both deserve good things.

5. I will say what I really think, even if my voice squeaks and my knees shake. Even if my words hurt you, I will do my best to be honest, believing that honesty brings intimacy.

6. I will let you feel your feelings without making them my feelings. You are allowed to feel happy, sad, angry,

or confused. Instead of trying to fix things or cheer you up, I will just sit beside you and listen.

7. I will feel my feelings, honoring my joy and my tears and believing that my feelings matter. I'll let myself get angry, laugh a little too loud, and cry, even if my face scrunches up.

8. I will accept my dimpled thighs and soft tummy, knowing that I am beautiful just as I am—knowing that my beauty runs much deeper than my physical body. My beauty, my uniqueness, comes from deep inside my heart.

9. I will commit to personal growth, to knowing myself better, and to becoming more whole. I'll meet with a therapist, read books, attend workshops, and surround myself with people who encourage me to be my best self.

10. I will speak kind words to myself, forgiving myself when I make mistakes and celebrating myself with each accomplishment. I will be my biggest fan.

11. I will bravely love myself, believing that I deserve love, believing that I am loved, right now. Bravely loving myself provides a solid foundation for me to love others with a whole heart.

ACKNOWLEDGMENTS

Thank you, reader, for journeying with me. It's been a journey unlike anything I expected—harder and so much better. I hope our paths cross in real life and I get to hear your story.

Thank you, Facebook friends and Instagram community and blog readers. This book exists because of you and your encouragement. You're amazing!

Thank you, Leonard Group team. Our business works because it's supported by incredibly talented people.

Thank you, Ori, for being a true partner. Steve and I love working with you.

Thank you to my coffee girls, Jen and Brenda. Our weekly chats over coffee are one of my favorite parts of the week.

Thank you to my coaches—Jim, who helped me discover I actually wanted to write a book, and Sara, who walked beside me page by page.

Thank you to my agent, Lisa, who reached out at just the right time. You had a vision for this book, and I'm grateful!

Thank you, *Brave Love* launch team. You were a huge part of getting this book out into the world. Thank you, Anna, for your passion in heading up the team.

Thank you to my Zondervan team. I am grateful to work with such a kind, smart, supportive group of people.

Thank you to my sisters—Chrissie, Susan, and Ellen. You are the people who love me no matter what, and I feel that love every minute.

Thank you, David, for teaching me what it looks like to love and accept oneself.

Thank you, Matthias, for showing me that creativity is bold and powerful and changes the world.

And thank you, Steve. You are my perfect partner—the one who is helping me grow. Your bravery inspires me. I love you.